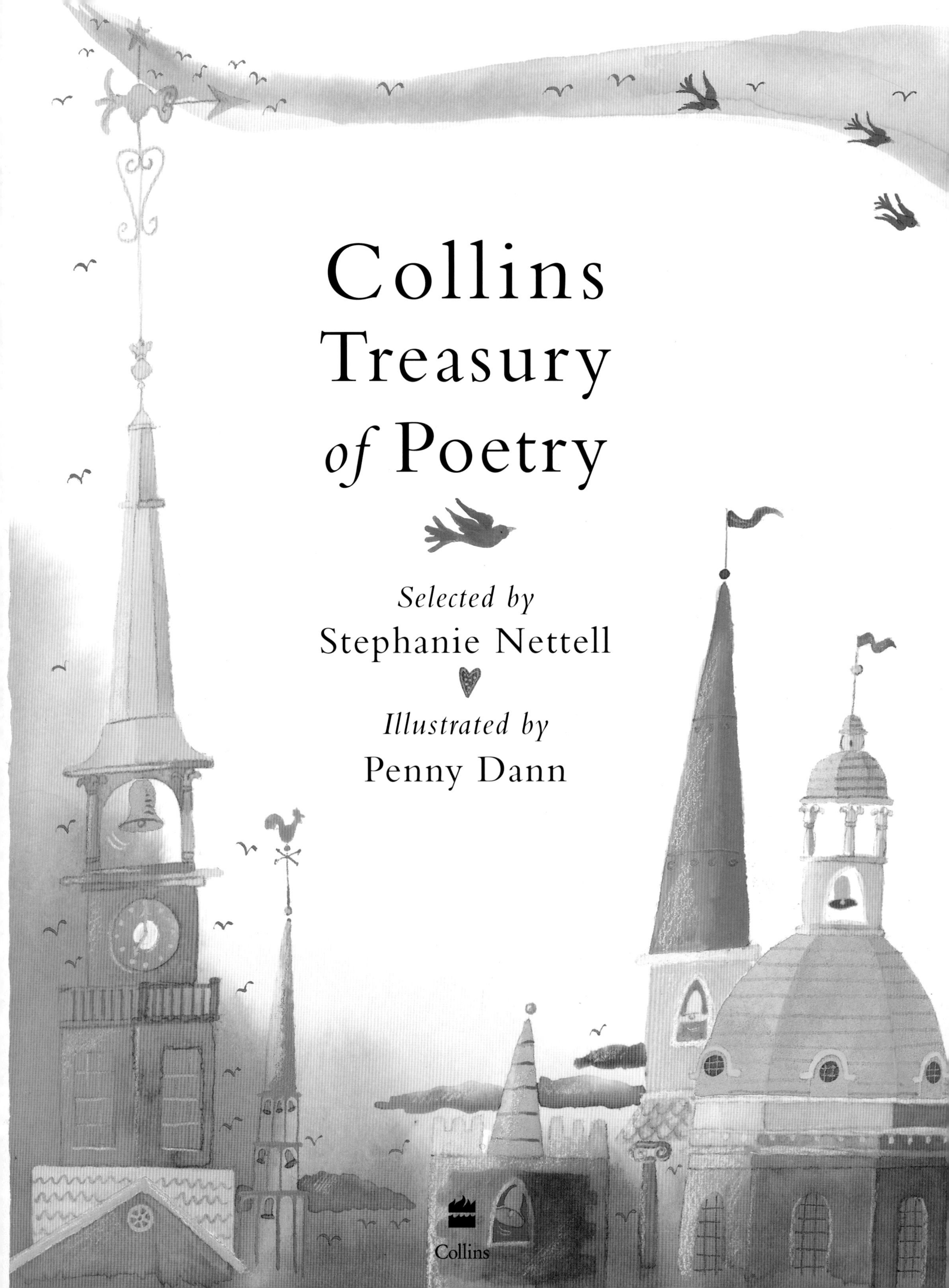

Collins Treasury *of* Poetry

Selected by

Stephanie Nettell

Illustrated by

Penny Dann

Collins

For Todd and Anna, 22 April 1995
S.N.
For J.D. with love
P.D.

First published in Great Britain by
HarperCollins Publishers Ltd in 1995
10 9 8 7 6 5 4 3 2 1

A CIP catalogue record for this title
is available from the British Library.

Printed and bound in Hong Kong.

Contents

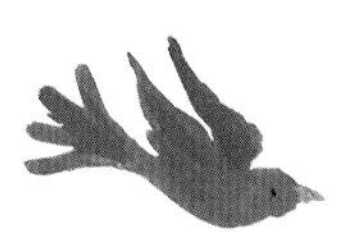

INTRODUCTION

An enticing volume of verse is as vital for a child as vitamin C. If we've encouraged a baby's instinctive pleasure in the sounds and rhythms of words, even before it could say any itself, it will quickly come to appreciate the potency of language. We'll have given it an essential power-tool for getting through life.

All very worthy – yet it doesn't explain why a book like this was such fun for me as an adult to compile and, I hope, for you to read.

The answer must lie in the joy of sharing a creepy story or a glistening landscape, a puzzle, a bouncy song or a piece of gobbledygook – especially if you're lucky enough to have a child to cuddle at the same time. Perhaps these verses allow us to go back to the world the young inhabit, one where everyday experiences are revelations and emotions fresh, one of gloriously simple jokes, of innocence and optimism.

Literature for centuries has taken it for granted we will catch its formal echoes of our childhood chants, but there is still a jolt of pleasure when we rediscover an actual rhyme and the long-ago memories it brings to life. So what I am offering here is an enduring collection of classic verse, from traditional sources and the familiarly revered as well as from contemporary poets – the seeds for a lifelong literary harvest.

Stephanie Nettell

Home Thoughts

Cottage

When I live in a Cottage
I shall keep in my Cottage
Two different Dogs
Three creamy Cows,
Four giddy Goats,
Five pewter Pots
Six silver Spoons
Seven busy Beehives
Eight ancient Appletrees
Nine red Rosebushes
Ten teeming Teapots
Eleven chirping Chickens
Twelve cosy Cats with their kittenish Kittens
and
One blessèd Baby in a Basket.
That's what I'll have when I live in my Cottage

ELEANOR FARJEON

Just When...

It's always the same.
Just when you're playing a game;
Just when it's exciting
And interesting
With everyone racing
And chasing,
Just when you're having so much fun,
Somebody always wants something done.

MAX FATCHEN

The Window

Behind the blinds I sit and watch
The people passing – passing by;
And not a single one can see
My tiny watching eye.

They cannot see my little room,
All yellowed with the shaded sun,
They do not even know I'm here;
Nor'll guess when I am gone.

WALTER DE LA MARE

In the Street

The fat old pillar-box in the street
Has a red and black jersey down to its feet
And keeps its big mouth open wide
To take the letters into its inside.

In the evening in the cold and damp
On one long leg stands the new street lamp.
High above us in its beak it holds
A golden fish it caught in the road.

The light at the crossing goes in and out
As if someone were blowing up
And letting down a round balloon
Or switching on and off the moon.

STANLEY COOK

Come on into my Tropical Garden

Come on into my tropical garden
Come on in and have a laugh in
Taste my sugar cake and my pine drink
Come on in please come on in

And yes you can stand up in my hammock
and breeze out in my trees
you can pick my hibiscus
and kiss my chimpanzees

O you can roll up in the grass
and if you pick up a flea
I'll take you down for a quick dip-wash
in the sea
believe me there's nothing better
for getting rid of a flea
than having a quick dip-wash in the sea

Come on into my tropical garden
Come on in please come on in

GRACE NICHOLS

This is Just to Say

I have eaten
the plums
that were in
the icebox

and which
you were probably
saving
for breakfast

Forgive me
they were delicious
so sweet
and so cold

WILLIAM CARLOS WILLIAMS

Peas

I eat my peas with honey,
I've done it all my life;
It makes the peas taste funny,
But it keeps them on the knife.

ANON

Colouring

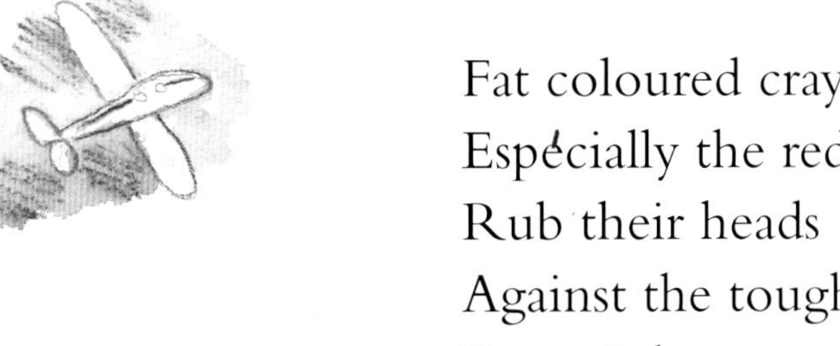

Fat coloured crayons
Especially the red ones,
Rub their heads
Against the tough grey
Paper I draw on
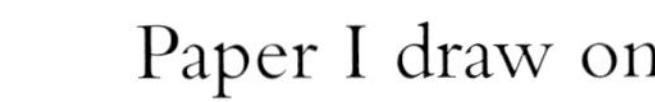

On my table;
And thick black pencils

In wooden jackets
Rub their noses in books.

Paintbrushes dip
Their tongues in colours

And take long licks
At children's pictures
Pinned to easels;
And even my fingers
Want to put
Themselves in the paint
And make red marks
All over my work.

STANLEY COOK

Mum

Mum'll be coming home today.
It's three weeks she's been away.
When Dad's alone
all we eat
is cold meat
which I don't like
and he burns the toast I want just-brown
and I hate taking the ash-can down.

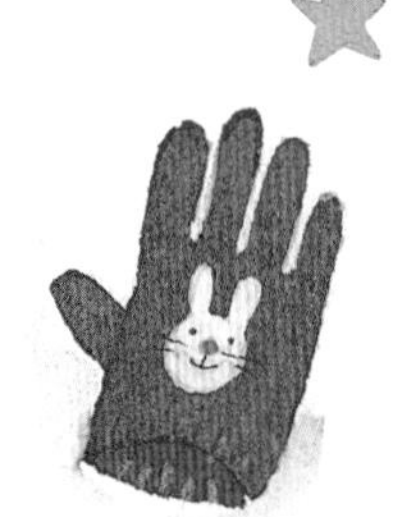

He's mended the door
from the little fight
on Thursday night
so it doesn't show
and can we have grilled tomatoes
Spanish onions and roast potatoes
and will you sing me "I'll never more roam"
when I'm in bed, when you've come home.

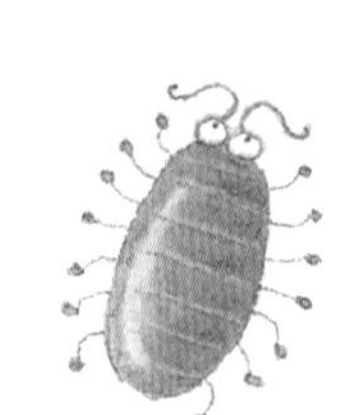

MICHAEL ROSEN

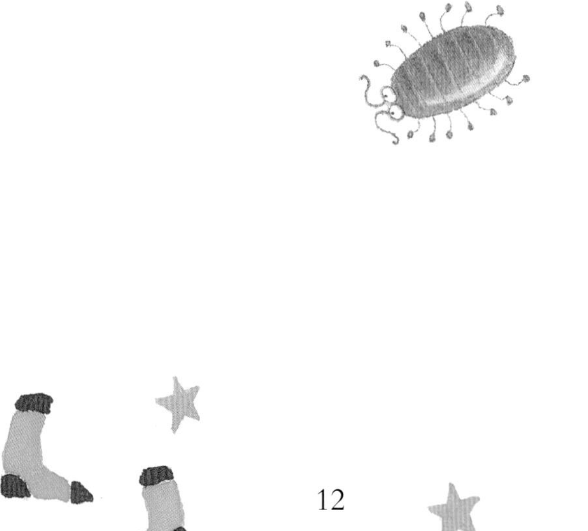

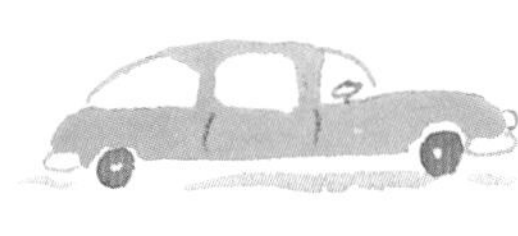
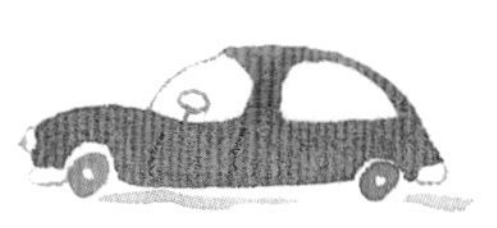

To Pass the Time

When I'm bored I count things:
Cornflakes, cars,
Pencils, people, leaves on trees,
Raindrops, stars,
Footsteps, heartbeats, pebbles, waves,
Gaggles, herds and flocks,
Freckles, blinks per minute,
The ticks
Of clocks.

Eighty-seven lamp-posts
Line our street.
Did you know a woodlouse has
Fourteen feet?
And – three vests, four pairs of pants, six shirts, two
T-shirts, one pair of jeans, two other pairs of trousers,
one pair of shorts, two belts, three pullovers (one of them
without sleeves), a raincoat, a jacket, two pairs of pyjamas,
one glove, one tie and eleven socks are
The clothes I've got
In five drawers and one wardrobe:
I'm bored
A lot.

RICHARD EDWARDS

sleep

it was dark but when i blinked
twice i could see all the way deep
into the forest
and the lion came at me
and i really took care of him (pooped him twice
in the nose)
then a big rhinoceros with purple dots
and bright pink eyes
and i flung him over my head and threw
him into his mother's lap (where he belongs
since i'm so badddd)
then this striped horse neighed
up on his hind feet
but i jumped high and bit his ear
and he ran away crying
also the big bird whose wings blotched
out the moonlight swooped down
on me and i tickled his feet
just before the talons sunk in
and he laughed and laughed and slapped me
on the back and went home
so it's easy to see when the rat climbed
into my bed how tired
i was and why i called
  moooooooommmmmmmmmmiiiiiiieeeeeeeeeeee

NIKKI GIOVANNI

FUN AND
* FANTASY *

The Man from the Land of Fandango

The man from the land of Fandango
Is coming to pay you a call,
With his tricolour jacket and polka-dot tie
And his calico trousers as blue as the sky
And a hat with a tassel and all.
And he bingles and bangles and bounces,
He's a bird! He's a bell! He's a ball!
The man from the land of Fandango
Is coming to pay you a call.
Oh, whenever they dance in Fandango
The bears and the bison join in,
And the baboons with bassoons make a musical sound,
And the kangaroos come with a hop and a bound,
And the dinosaurs join in the din,
And they tingle and tongle and tangle
Till tomorrow turns into today.
Then they stop for a break and a drink and a cake
In their friendly fandandical way.

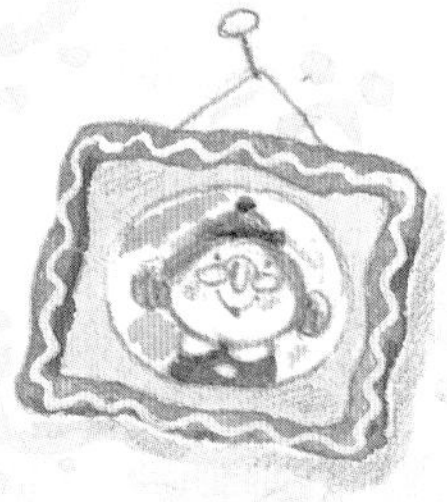

The man from the land of Fandango
Is given to dancing and dreams.
He comes in at the door like a somersault star
And he juggles with junkets and jam in a jar
And custards and caramel creams.
And he jingles and jongles and jangles
As he dances on ceilings and walls,
And he appears every five hundred years
So you'd better be home when he calls.

MARGARET MAHY

Moon-Transport

Some people on the moon are so idle
They will not so much as saunter, much less sidle.

But if they cannot bear to walk, or try,
How do they get to the places where they lie?

They gather together, as people do for a bus.
"All aboard, whoever's coming with us."

Then they climb on to each other till they are all
Clinging in one enormous human ball.

Then they roll, and so, without lifting their feet,
Progress quite successfully down the street.

TED HUGHES

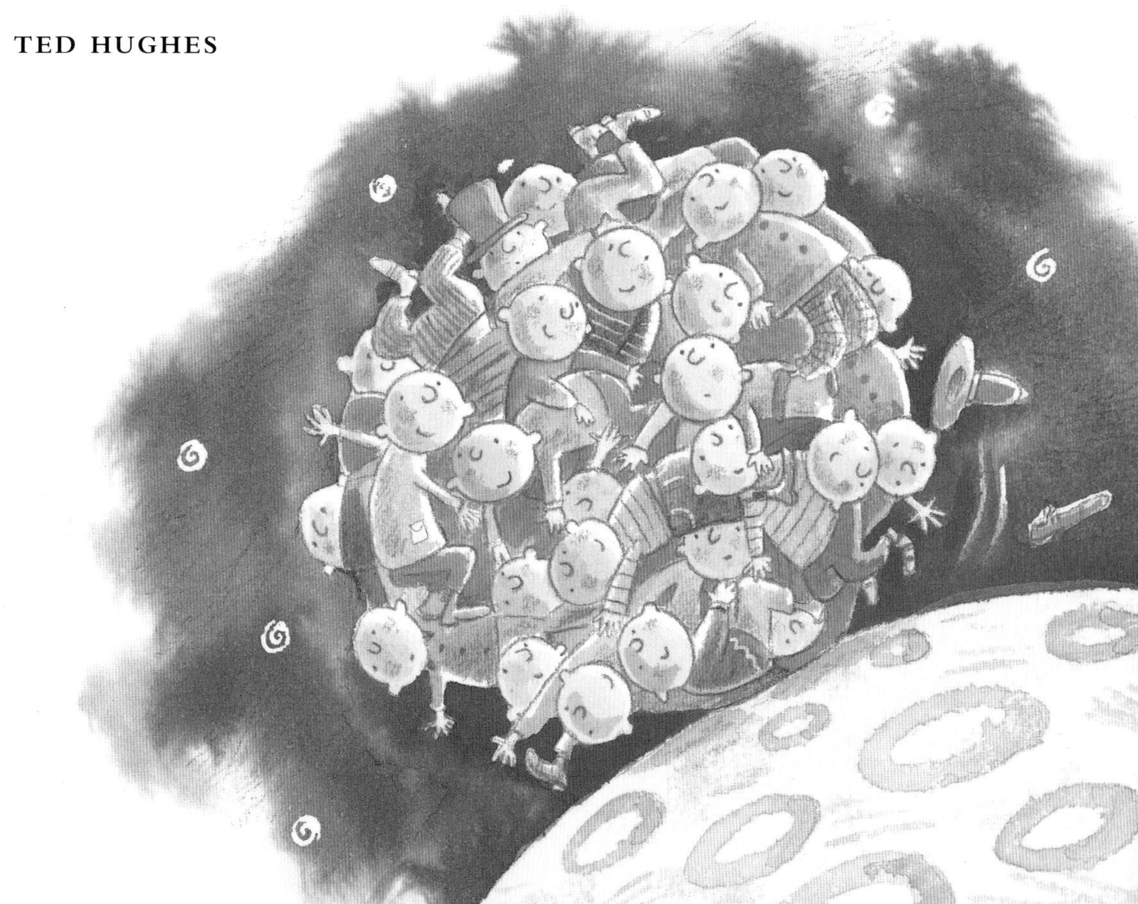

He was a Rat

He was a rat, and she was a rat,
And down in one hole they did dwell,
And both were as black as a witch's cat,
And they loved each other well.

He had a tail, and she had a tail,
Both long and curling and fine;
And each said, "Yours is the finest tail
In the world, excepting mine."

He smelt the cheese, and she smelt the cheese,
And they both pronounced it good;
And both remarked it would greatly add
To the charms of their daily food.

So he ventured out, and she ventured out,
And I saw them go with pain;
But what befell them I never can tell,
For they never came back again.

ANON

There was an Old Woman

There was an old woman tossed up in a basket
Nineteen times as high as the moon;
Where she was going I couldn't but ask it,
For in her hand she carried a broom.

"Old woman, old woman, old woman," quoth I,
"Oh whither, Oh whither, Oh whither, so high?"
"To brush the cobwebs off the sky!"
"Shall I go with thee?" "Ay, by-and-by."

ANON

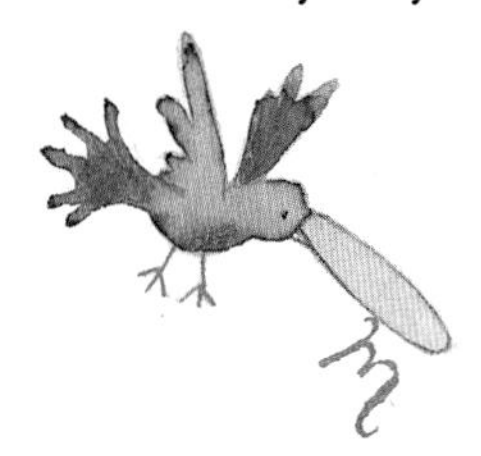

Tree-Disease

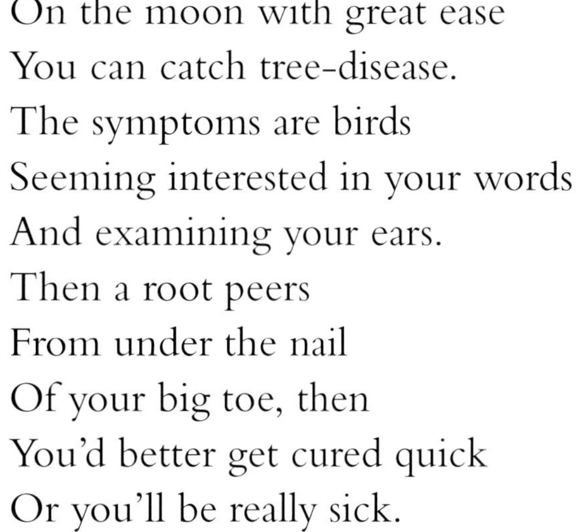

On the moon with great ease
You can catch tree-disease.
The symptoms are birds
Seeming interested in your words
And examining your ears.
Then a root peers
From under the nail
Of your big toe, then
You'd better get cured quick
Or you'll be really sick.

TED HUGHES

Wynken, Blynken, and Nod

Wynken, Blynken, and Nod one night
Sailed off in a wooden shoe –
Sailed on a river of crystal light,
Into a sea of dew.
"Where are you going and what do you wish?"
The old moon asked the three.
"We have come to fish for the herring-fish
That live in this beautiful sea;
Nets of silver and gold have we,"
Said Wynken, Blynken, and Nod.

The old moon laughed and sang a song,
As they rocked in the wooden shoe,
And the wind that sped them all night long
Ruffled the waves of dew.
The little stars were the herring-fish
That lived in that beautiful sea –
"Now cast your nets wherever you wish –
But never afeared are we";
So cried the stars to the fishermen three:
Wynken, Blynken, and Nod.

All night long their nets they threw
To the stars in the twinkling foam –
Then down from the skies came the wooden shoe,
Bringing the fishermen home;
'Twas all so pretty a sail, it seemed
As if it could not be,
And some folks thought 'twas a dream they'd dreamed
Of sailing the beautiful sea –
But I shall name you the fishermen three:
Wynken, Blynken, and Nod.

Wynken and Blynken are two little eyes,
And Nod is a little head,
And the wooden shoe that sailed the skies
Is a wee one's trundle-bed.
So shut your eyes while mother sings
Of wonderful sights that be,
And you shall see the beautiful things
As you rock on the misty sea,
Where the old shoe rocked the fishermen three:
Wynken, Blynken, and Nod.

EUGENE FIELD

The Magic Seeds

There was an old woman who sowed a corn seed,
And from it there sprouted a tall yellow weed.
She planted the seeds of the tall yellow flower,
And up sprang a blue one in less than an hour,
The seed of the blue one she sowed in a bed,
And up sprang a tall tree with blossoms of red.
And high in the treetop there sang a white bird,
And his song was the sweetest that ever was heard.
The people they came from far and from near,
The song of the little white bird for to hear.

JAMES REEVES

Not a Very Cheerful Song, I'm Afraid

There was a gloomy lady,
With a gloomy duck and a gloomy drake,
And they all three wandered gloomily,
Beside a gloomy lake,
On a gloomy, gloomy, gloomy, gloomy, gloomy, gloomy day.

Now underneath that gloomy lake
The gloomy lady's gone.
But the gloomy duck and the gloomy drake
Swim on and on and on,
On a gloomy, gloomy, gloomy, gloomy, gloomy, gloomy day.

ADRIAN MITCHELL

The Owl and the Pussy-Cat

I

The Owl and the Pussy-Cat went to sea
  In a beautiful pea-green boat,
They took some honey, and plenty of money,
  Wrapped up in a five-pound note.
The Owl looked up to the stars above,
  And sang to a small guitar,
"O lovely Pussy! O Pussy, my love,
  "What a beautiful Pussy you are,
      "You are,
      "You are!
  "What a beautiful Pussy you are!"

II

Pussy said to the Owl, "You elegant fowl!
  "How charmingly sweet you sing!
"O let us be married! too long we have tarried:
  "But what shall we do for a ring?"
They sailed away for a year and a day,
  To the land where the Bong-Tree grows,
And there in a wood a Piggy-wig stood,
  With a ring at the end of his nose,
      His nose,
      His nose,
  With a ring at the end of his nose.

III

“Dear Pig, are you willing to sell for one shilling
    “Your ring?” Said the Piggy, “I will.”
So they took it away, and were married next day
    By the Turkey who lives on the hill.
They dined on mince, and slices of quince,
    Which they ate with a runcible spoon;
And hand in hand, on the edge of the sand,
    They danced by the light of the moon,
        The moon,
        The moon,
    They danced by the light of the moon.

EDWARD LEAR

Mr Blob

My heart went out to Mr Blob the moment that we met,
And the manner of his coming is a thing I can't forget.
It fell upon a Sunday in the merry month of June,
Between a rainy morning and a rainy afternoon.

He didn't use the window, and he didn't use the door;
He never took his hat off, and he never touched the floor;
He didn't look as if he'd grown, like us: he just began,
And he stood before us there, a simple English gentleman.

He wasn't very dandified or dainty in his dress,
But the absence of his trousers seemed to cause him no distress,
For the smile upon his features was a marvel to behold,
And underneath that buttoned vest there beat a heart of gold.

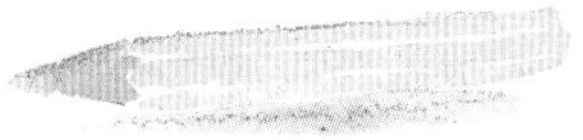

He wasn't long among us: all too little had been said
When a heavy hand descended on his inoffensive head,
And a Voice delivered judgement: "Mr Blob is far too stout;
He's a silly little fellow, and I mean to rub him out."

He didn't seem offended, but I think he must have heard,
For he rose up from the paper and he went without a word.
His boots and buttons only lingered on a little while,
And the last of him to vanish was the vestige of a smile.

O Mr Blob, the world would be a very pleasant place
If everyone resembled you in figure and in face.
If everybody went about with open arms like you
The stars would all be brighter and the sky a bluer blue.

My heart went out to Mr Blob the moment that we met,
And the sorrow of his going is a thing that haunts me yet;
For often when the clouds are low I sit at home and sob
To think that I shall see no more the face of Mr Blob.

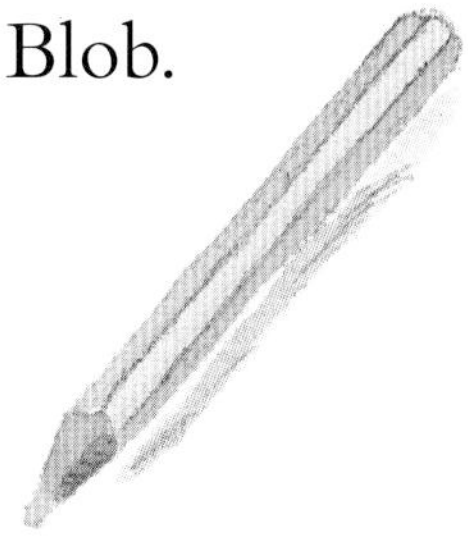

E.V. RIEU

The King of China's Daughter

The King of China's daughter,
She never would love me
Though I hung my cap and bells upon
Her nutmeg tree.
For oranges and lemons,
The stars in bright blue air
(I stole them long ago my dear),
Were dangling there.
The Moon did give me silver pence,
The Sun did give me gold,
And both together softly blew
And made my porridge cold;
But the King of China's daughter
Pretended not to see
When I hung my cap and bells upon
Her nutmeg tree.

The King of China's daughter,
So beautiful to see
With her face like yellow water
Left her nutmeg tree.
Her little rope for skipping
She kissed and gave it me
Made of painted notes of singing birds
Among the fields of tea.
I skipped across the nutmeg field
I skipped across the sea
And neither sun nor moon my dear
Has yet caught me.

EDITH SITWELL

The Key of the Kingdom

This is the Key of the Kingdom:
In that Kingdom there is a city;
In that city is a town;
In that town there is a street;
In that street there winds a lane;
In that lane there is a yard;
In that yard there is a house;
In that house there waits a room;
In that room an empty bed;
And on that bed a basket –
A basket of sweet flowers:
Of flowers, of flowers;
A basket of sweet flowers.

Flowers in a basket;
Basket on the bed;
Bed in the chamber;
Chamber in the house;
House in the weedy yard;
Yard in the winding lane;
Lane in the broad street;
Street in the high town;
Town in the city;
City in the Kingdom –
This is the Key of the Kingdom.
Of the Kingdom this is the Key.

ANON

SUNSHINE AND SHOWERS

Snow

No breath of wind,
No gleam of sun –
Still the white snow
Whirls softly down –
Twig and bough
And blade and thorn
All in an icy
Quiet, forlorn.
Whispering, rustling,
Through the air,
On sill and stone,
Roof – everywhere,
It heaps its powdery
Crystal flakes,
Of every tree
A mountain makes;
Till pale and faint
At shut of day,
Stoops from the West
One wintry ray.
And feathered in fire,
Where ghosts the moon,
A robin shrills
His lonely tune.

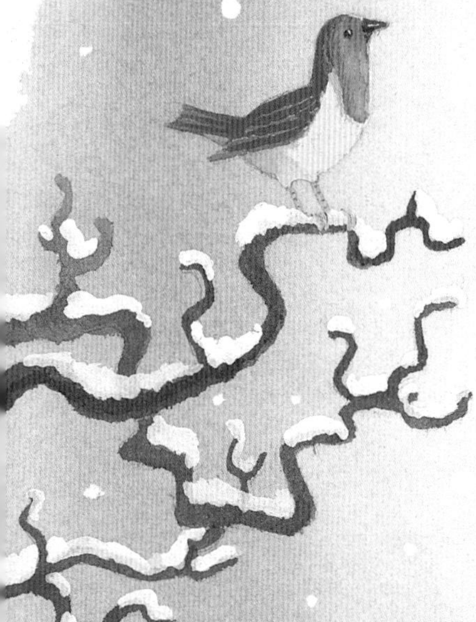

WALTER DE LA MARE

The Wind in the Grass

The green grass is bowing,
The morning wind is in it,
'Tis a tune worth thy knowing,
Though it change every minute.

RALPH W. EMERSON

The Rain

I hear leaves drinking Rain;
I hear rich leaves on top
Giving the poor beneath
Drop after drop;
'Tis a sweet noise to hear
These green leaves drinking near.

And when the Sun comes out,
After this Rain shall stop,
A wondrous Light will fill
Each dark, round drop;
I hope the Sun shines bright:
'Twill be a lovely sight.

W.H. DAVIES

Weather

Dot a dot dot dot a dot dot
Spotting the windowpane.

Spack a spack speck flick a flack fleck
Freckling the windowpane.

A spatter a scatter a wet cat a clatter
A splatter a rumble outside.

Umbrella umbrella umbrella umbrella
Bumbershoot barrell of rain.

Slosh a galosh slosh a galosh
Slither and slather a glide

A puddle a jump a puddle a jump
A puddle a jump puddle splosh

A juddle a pump a luddle a dump
A pudmuddle jump in and slide!

EVE MERRIAM

Fog

The fog comes
on little cat feet.
It sits looking

over harbour and city
on silent haunches
and then moves on.

CARL SANDBURG

Chips

Out of the paper bag
Comes the hot breath of the chips
And I shall blow on them
To stop them burning my lips.

Before I leave the counter
The woman shakes
Raindrops of vinegar on them
And salty snowflakes.

Outside the frosty pavements
Are slippery as a slide
But the chips and I
Are warm inside.

STANLEY COOK

I am the Rain

I am the rain
I like to play games
like sometimes
    I pretend
I'm going
    to fall
Man, that's the time
I don't come at all

Like sometimes
I get these laughing stitches
up my sides
    rushing people in
and out
    with the clothesline
I just love drip
    dropping
down collars
    and spines
Maybe it's a shame
but it's the only way
I get some fame

GRACE NICHOLS

SEASONS' GREETINGS

springtime

in springtime the violets
grow in the sidewalk cracks
and the ants play furiously
at my gym-shoed toes
carrying off a half-eaten peanut
butter sandwich i had at lunch
and sometimes i crumble
my extra graham crackers
and on the rainy days i take off
my yellow space hat and splash
all the puddles on Pendry Street and not one
cold can catch me

NIKKI GIOVANNI

Pippa's Song

The year's at the spring;
The day's at the morn;
Morning's at seven;
The hill-side's dew-pearled;
The lark's on the wing;
The snail's on the thorn;
God's in His heaven –
All's right with the world!

ROBERT BROWNING

Child's Song in Spring

The silver birch is a dainty lady,
She wears a satin gown;
The elm-tree makes the churchyard shady,
She will not live in town.

The English oak is a sturdy fellow;
He gets his green coat late;
The willow is smart in a suit of yellow,
While brown the beech trees wait.

Such a gay green gown God gives the larches –
As green as He is good!
The hazels hold up their arms for arches
When Spring rides through the wood.

The chestnut's proud, and the lilac's pretty,
The poplar's gentle and tall,
But the plane tree's kind to the poor dull city –
I love him best of all!

E. NESBIT

little tree
little silent Christmas tree
you are so little
you are more like a flower

who found you in the green forest
and were you very sorry to come away?
see   i will comfort you
because you smell so sweetly

i will kiss your cool bark
and hug you safe and tight
just as your mother would,
only don't be afraid

look   the spangles
that sleep all the year in a dark box
dreaming of being taken out and allowed to shine,
the balls the chains red and gold the fluffy threads,

put up your little arms
and i'll give them all to you to hold
every finger shall have its ring
and there won't be a single place dark or unhappy

then when you're quite dressed
you'll stand in the window for everyone to see
and how they'll stare!
oh but you'll be very proud

and my little sister and i will take hands
and looking up at our beautiful tree
we'll dance and sing
"Noel Noel"

e.e. cummings

The Waiting Game

Nuts and marbles in the toe,
An orange in the heel,
A Christmas stocking in the dark
Is wonderful to feel.

Shadowy, bulging length of leg
That crackles when you clutch,
A Christmas stocking in the dark
Is marvellous to touch.

You lie back on your pillow
But that shape's still hanging there.
A Christmas stocking in the dark
Is very hard to bear,

So try to get to sleep again
And chase the hours away.
A Christmas stocking in the dark
Must wait for Christmas Day.

JOHN MOLE

Creatures Great and Small

Animals' Houses

Of animals' houses
  Two sorts are found –
Those which are square ones
  And those which are round.

Square is a hen-house,
  A kennel, a sty:
Cows have square houses
  And so have I.

A snail's shell is curly,
  A bird's nest round;
Rabbits have twisty burrows
  Underground.

But the fish in the bowl
  And the fish at sea –
Their houses are round
  As a house can be.

JAMES REEVES

The City Mouse and the Garden Mouse

The city mouse lives in a house;
The garden mouse lives in a bower,
He's friendly with the frogs and toads,
And sees the pretty plants in flower.

The city mouse eats bread and cheese;
The garden mouse eats what he can;
We will not grudge him seeds and stocks,
Poor little timid furry man.

CHRISTINA ROSSETTI

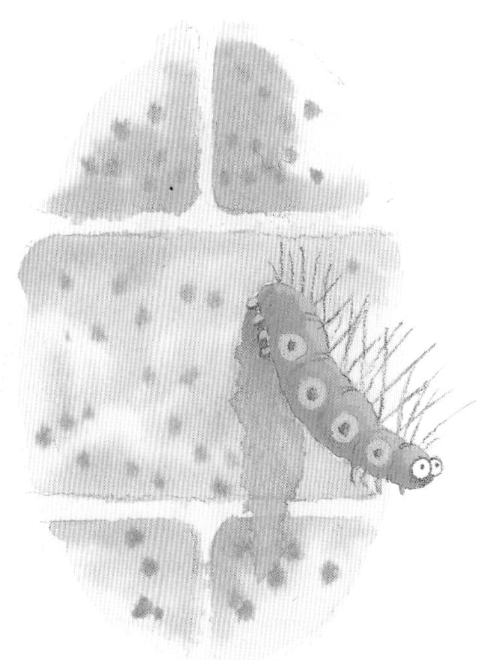

The Tickle Rhyme

"Who's that tickling my back?" said the wall.
"Me," said a small
Caterpillar. "I'm learning
To crawl."

IAN SERRAILLIER

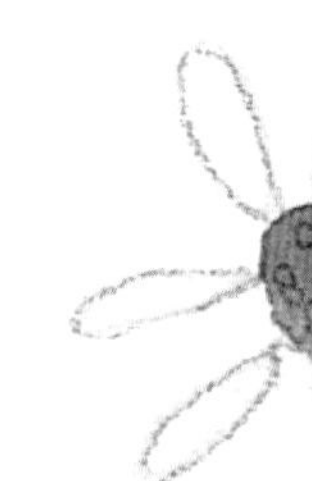

Squirrel

With a rocketing rip
Squirrel will zip
Up a tree-bole
As if down a hole.

He jars to a stop
With tingling ears.
He has two gears:
Freeze and top.

Then up again, plucky
As a jockey
Galloping a Race-
-Horse into space.

TED HUGHES

Algy

Algy met a bear,
A bear met Algy.
The bear was bulgy,
The bulge was Algy.

ANON

The Caterpillar

Brown and furry
Caterpillar in a hurry,
Take your walk
To the shady leaf, or stalk,
Or what not,
Which may be the chosen spot.
No toad spy you,
Hovering bird of prey pass by you;
Spin and die,
To live again a butterfly.

CHRISTINA ROSSETTI

The Snare

I hear a sudden cry of pain!
There is a rabbit in a snare:
Now I hear the cry again,
But I cannot tell from where.

But I cannot tell from where
He is calling out for aid;
Crying on the frightened air,
Making everything afraid.

Making everything afraid,
Wrinkling up his little face,
As he cries again for aid;
And I cannot find the place!

And I cannot find the place
Where his paw is in the snare:
Little one! Oh, little one!
I am searching everywhere.

JAMES STEPHENS

Hide and Seek

Looking for Daisy
This way and that,
Try in the hayloft:
"Miaow," says the cat.

Looking for Daisy,
Haven't a clue,
Try in the farmyard:
The cow says, "Moo."

Looking for Daisy
All round the house,
Try in the cellar:
"Squeak," says the mouse.

Looking for Daisy,
Quite out of puff,
Try in the kennel:
The dog says, "Ruff."

Looking for Daisy,
Oh, help me, please!
Try in the garden:
"Buzz," say the bees.

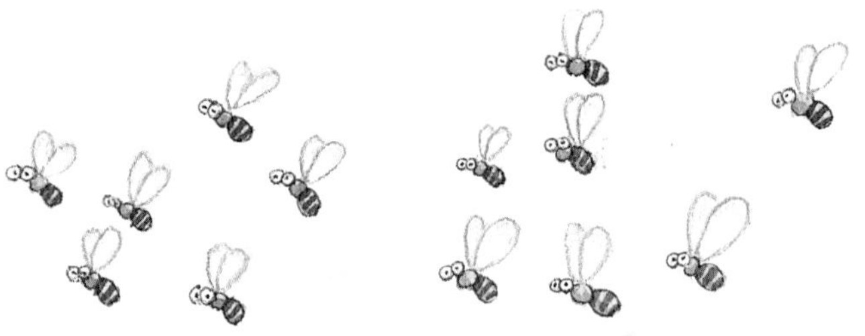

Looking for Daisy
Most of the day,
Try in the stable:
The horse says: "Neigh."

Looking for Daisy,
Where did she go!
Sitting and thinking:
Suddenly, "Bo!"

"Daisy! Oh, Daisy!
I must have walked miles.
Where were you hiding?"
Daisy just smiles.

RICHARD EDWARDS

My Dog

My dog is such a gentle soul,
Although he's big it's true.
He brings the paper in his mouth.
He brings the postman too.

MAX FATCHEN

The Little Black Hen

Berryman and Baxter,
  Prettiboy and Penn
And old Farmer Middleton
  Are five big men...
And all of them were after
  The Little Black Hen.

She ran quickly,
  They ran fast;
Baxter was first, and
  Berryman was last.
I sat and watched
  By the old plum-tree...
She squawked through the hedge
  And she came to me.

The Little Black Hen
  Said, "Oh, it's you!"
I said, "Thank you,
  How do you do?
And please will you tell me,
  Little Black Hen,
What did they want,
  Those five big men?"

The Little Black Hen
  She said to me:
"They want me to lay them
  An egg for tea.
If they were Emperors,
  If they were Kings,
I'm much too busy
  To lay them things."

"I'm not a King
  And I haven't a crown:
I climb up trees,
  And I tumble down.
I can shut one eye,
  I can count to ten,
So lay me an egg, please,
  Little Black Hen."

The Little Black Hen said,
  "What will you pay,
If I lay you an egg
  For Easter Day?"

"I'll give you a Please
And a How-do-you-do,
I'll show you a Bear
Who lives in the Zoo,
I'll show you the nettle-place
On my leg,
If you'll lay me a great big
Eastery egg."

The Little Black Hen
Said, "I don't care
For a How-do-you-do
Or a Big-brown-bear,
But I'll lay you a beautiful
Eastery egg,
If you'll show me the nettle-place
On your leg."

I showed her the place
Where I had my sting.
She touched it gently
With one black wing.
"Nettles don't hurt
If you count to ten.
And now for the egg,"
Said the Little Black Hen.

When I wake up
On Easter Day,
I shall see my egg
She's promised to lay.
If I were Emperors,
If I were Kings,
It couldn't be fuller
Of wonderful things.

Berryman and Baxter,
Prettiboy and Penn,
And old Farmer Middleton
Are five big men.
All of them are wanting
An egg for their tea,
But the Little Black Hen is much too busy,
The Little Black Hen is *much* too busy,
The Little Black Hen is MUCH too busy...
She's laying my egg for me!

A.A. MILNE

Who's There?

Knock, knock!
Who's there?
cried the spider.
Stand and wait!
But she knew by the
gentle tweak of the web
it was her mate.

Knock, knock!
Who's there?
cried the spider.
Call your name!
But she knew by the
soft tap-tap on the silk
her spiderlings came.

Knock, knock!
Who's there?
cried the spider.
Who goes by?
But she knew by the
shaking of her net
it was the fly.

JUDITH NICHOLLS

Spin Me a Web, Spider

Spin me a web, spider,
Across the window-pane
For I shall never break it
And make you start again.

Cast your net of silver
As soon as it is spun,
And hang it with the morning dew
That glitters in the sun.

It's strung with pearls and diamonds,
The finest ever seen,
Fit for any royal King
Or any royal Queen.

Would you, could you, bring it down
In the dust to lie?
Any day of the week, my dear,
Said the nimble fly.

CHARLES CAUSLEY

Worm

Lowly, slowly,
A pink, wet worm
Sings in the rain:
O see me squirm

Along the path.
I warp and wind.
I'm searching hard.
If I could find

My elbow, my hair,
My hat, my shoe,
I'd look as pretty
As you, and you.

TED HUGHES

Cow

The Cow comes home swinging
Her udder and singing:

"The dirt O the dirt
It does me no hurt.

And a good splash of muck
Is a blessing of luck.

O I splosh through the mud
But the breath of my cud

Is sweeter than silk.
O I splush through manure

But my heart stays pure
As a pitcher of milk."

TED HUGHES

Cat Warmth

All afternoon,
My cat sleeps,
On the end of my bed.

When I creep my toes
Down between the cold sheets,
I find a patch of cat-warmth
That he's left behind;
An invisible gift.

JOHN CUNLIFFE

Cat in the Dark

Look at that!
Look at that!

But when you look
there's no cat.

Without a purr
just a flash of fur
and gone
like a ghost.

The most
you see
are two tiny
green traffic lights
staring at the night.

JOHN AGARD

The Three Little Kittens

Three little kittens lost their mittens;
And they began to cry,
"Oh, mother dear,
We very much fear
That we have lost our mittens."
"Lost your mittens!
You naughty kittens!
Then you shall have no pie!"
"Mee-ow, mee-ow, mee-ow."
"No, you shall have no pie."
"Mee-ow, mee-ow, mee-ow."

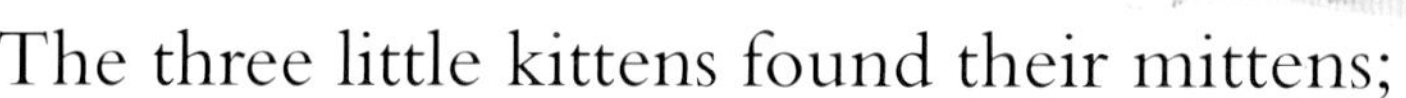

The three little kittens found their mittens;
And they began to cry,
"Oh, mother dear,
See here, see here!
See, we have found our mittens!"
"Put on your mittens,
You silly kittens,
And you may have some pie."
"Purr-r, purr-r, purr-r,
Oh, let us have the pie!
Purr-r, purr-r, purr-r."

The three little kittens put on their mittens,
And soon ate up the pie;
    "Oh, mother dear,
    We greatly fear
That we have soiled our mittens!"
    "Soiled your mittens!
    You naughty kittens!"
Then they began to sigh,
    "Mee-ow, mee-ow, mee-ow."
Then they began to sigh,
    "Mee-ow, mee-ow, mee-ow."

The three little kittens washed their mittens,
And hung them out to dry;
    "Oh, mother dear,
    Do not you hear
That we have washed our mittens?"
    "Washed your mittens!
    Oh, you're good kittens!
But I smell a rat close by,
    Hush, hush! Mee-ow, mee-ow."
"We smell a rat close by,
    Mee-ow, mee-ow, mee-ow."

ELIZA LEE FOLLEN

Choosing their Names

Our old cat has kittens three –
What do you think their names should be?

One is a tabby, with emerald eyes,
  And a tail that's long and slender,
And into a temper she quickly flies
  If you ever by chance offend her:
    I think we shall call her this –
    I think we shall call her that –
Now, don't you think that Pepperpot
  Is a nice name for a cat?

One is black, with a frill of white,
  And her feet are all white fur, too;
If you stroke her she carries her tail upright
  And quickly begins to purr, too!
    I think we shall call her this –
    I think we shall call her that –
Now don't you think that Sootikin
  Is a nice name for a cat?

One is a tortoise-shell, yellow and black,
  With plenty of white about him;
If you tease him, at once he sets up his back:
  He's a quarrelsome one, ne'er doubt him.
    I think we shall call him this –
    I think we shall call him that –
Now don't you think that Scratchaway
  Is a nice name for a cat?

Our old cat has kittens three
And I fancy these their names will be;
Pepperpot, Sootikin, Scratchaway – there!
Were ever kittens with these to compare?
And we call the old mother –
Now, what do you think?
Tabitha Longclaws Tiddley Wink.

THOMAS HOOD

Little Fish

The tiny fish enjoy themselves
in the sea.
Quick little splinters of life,
their little lives are fun to them
in the sea.

D.H. LAWRENCE

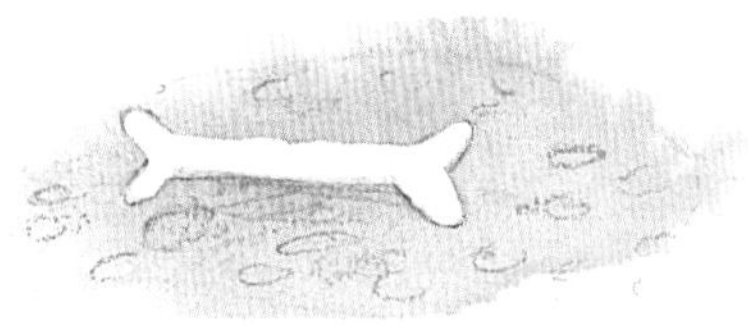

Lone Dog

I'm a lean dog, a keen dog, a wild dog and lone,
I'm a rough dog, a tough dog, hunting on my own!
I'm a bad dog, a mad dog, teasing silly sheep;
I love to sit and bay at the moon and keep fat souls from sleep.

I'll never be a lap dog, licking dirty feet,
A sleek dog, a meek dog, cringing for my meat.
Not for me the fireside, the well-filled plate,
But shut the door and sharp stone and cuff and kick and hate.

Not for me the other dogs, running by my side,
Some have run a short while, but none of them would bide.
O mine is still the lone trail, the hard trail, the best,
Wide wind and wild stars and the hunger of the quest.

IRENE McLEOD

Mrs Christmas

She was about as small as a cup
But big as your hand when she grew up
And she came to stay on Christmas Day
So we called her Mrs Christmas.

She liked to swoop around the hall
With a silver paper soccer ball
And I think I was four but maybe some more
When I named her Mrs Christmas.

She had some kittens with bright white socks
And she kept them out in a brown cardboard box
And she'd nudge them out and march them about
Saying: "I am Mrs Christmas".

ADRIAN MITCHELL

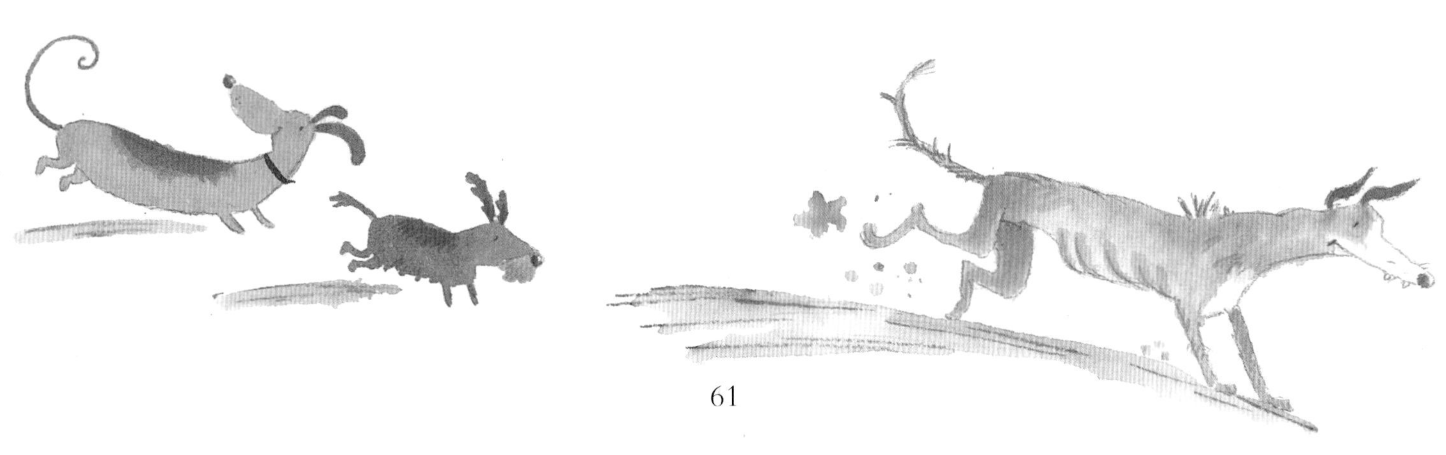

Duck's Ditty

All along the backwater,
Through the rushes tall,
Ducks are a-dabbling,
Up tails all!

Ducks' tails, drakes' tails,
Yellow feet a-quiver,
Yellow bills all out of sight
Busy in the river!

Slushy green undergrowth
Where the roach swim,
Here we keep our larder
Cool and full and dim!

Every one for what he likes!
We like to be
Heads down, tails up,
Dabbling free!

High in the blue above
Swifts whirl and call –
We are down a-dabbling,
Up tails all!

KENNETH GRAHAME

Little Trotty Wagtail

Little Trotty Wagtail, he went in the rain,
And twittering, tottering sideways he ne'er got straight again.
He stooped to get a worm, and looked up to get a fly,
And then he flew away ere his feathers they were dry.

Little Trotty Wagtail, he waddled in the mud,
And left his little footmarks, trample where he would.
He waddled in the water-pudge, and waggle went his tail,
And chirrupt up his wings to dry upon the garden rail.

Little Trotty Wagtail, you nimble all about,
And in the dimpling water-pudge you waddle in and out;
Your home is nigh at hand, and in the warm pig-stye,
So, little Master Wagtail, I'll bid you a good-bye.

JOHN CLARE

The Shark

A treacherous monster is the Shark
He never makes the least remark.

And when he sees you on the sand,
He doesn't seem to want to land.

He watches you take off your clothes,
And not the least excitement shows.

His eyes do not grow bright or roll,
He has astounding self-control.

He waits till you are quite undrest,
And seems to take no interest.

And when towards the sea you leap,
He looks as if he were asleep.

But when you once get in his range,
His whole demeanour seems to change.

He throws his body right about,
And his true character comes out.

It's no use crying or appealing,
He seems to lose all decent feeling.

After this warning you will wish
To keep clear of this treacherous fish.

His back is black, his stomach white,
He has a very dangerous bite.

LORD ALFRED DOUGLAS

A Horse and a Flea

A horse and a flea and three blind mice
Sat on a kerbstone shooting dice.
The horse he slipped and fell on the flea.
The flea said, "Whoops, there's a horse on me."

ANON

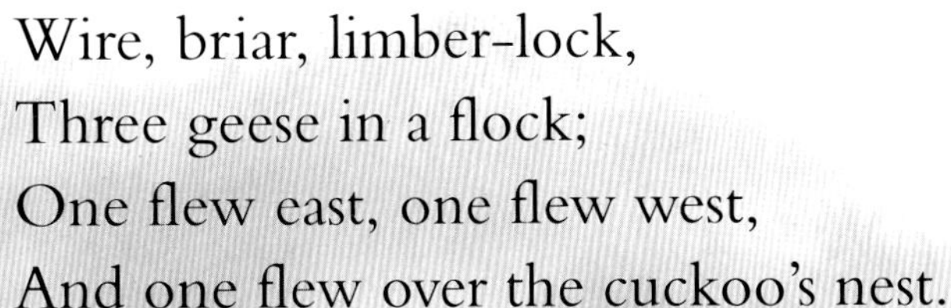

Wire, briar, limber-lock,
Three geese in a flock;
One flew east, one flew west,
And one flew over the cuckoo's nest.

ANON

Zebra

White men in Africa,
Puffing at their pipes,
Think the zebra's a white horse
With black stripes.

Black men in Africa,
With pipes of different types,
Know the zebra's a black horse
With white stripes.

GAVIN EWART

The Elephant

When people call this beast to mind,
  They marvel more and more
At such a little tail behind
  So LARGE a trunk before.

HILAIRE BELLOC

The Blackbird

"Sooty-plumed blackbird with your golden bill,
Why is your song so sweet and clear and mellow?"
"I lubricate my voice with slugs and snails."
"And sometimes cherries, too?" "Well, do you grudge me those –
Who pay you richly with a summer tune?"

JOHN HEATH-STUBBS

VERY SPECIAL PEOPLE

Granny Granny Please Comb my Hair

Granny Granny please comb my hair
you always take your time
you always take such care

You put me on a cushion between your knees
you rub a little coconut oil
parting gentle as a breeze

Mummy Mummy
she's always in a hurry-hurry
rush
she pulls my hair
sometimes she tugs

But Granny
you have all the time
in the world
and when you're finished
you always turn my head and say
"Now who's a nice girl?"

GRACE NICHOLS

Seumas Beg

A man was sitting underneath a tree
Outside the village; and he asked me what
Name was upon this place; and said that he
Was never here before – He told a lot

Of stories to me too. His nose was flat!
I asked him how it happened, and he said
– The first mate of the Holy Ghost did that
With a marling-spike one day; but he was dead,

And jolly good job too; and he'd have gone
A long way to have killed him – Oh, he had
A gold ring in one ear; the other one
– "Was bit off by a crocodile, bedad!"–

That's what he said. He taught me how to chew!
He was a real nice man! He liked me too!

JAMES STEPHENS

My Sister Jane

And I say nothing – no, not a word
About our Jane. Haven't you heard?
She's a bird, a bird, a bird, a bird.
Oh it never would do to let folks know
My sister's nothing but a great big crow.

Each day (we daren't send her to school)
She pulls on stockings of thick blue wool
To make her pin crow legs look right,
Then fits a wig of curls on tight,
And dark spectacles – a huge pair
To cover her very crowy stare.
Oh it never would do to let folks know
My sister's nothing but a great big crow.

When visitors come she sits upright
(With her wings and her tail tucked out of sight).
They think her queer but extremely polite.
Then when the visitors have gone
She whips out her wings and with her wig on
Whirls through the house at the height of your head –
Duck, duck, or she'll knock you dead.
Oh it never would do to let folks know
My sister's nothing but a great big crow.

At meals whatever she sees she'll stab it –
Because she's a crow and that's a crow habit.
My mother says "Jane! Your manners! Please!"
Then she'll sit quietly on the cheese,
Or play the piano nicely by dancing on the keys –
Oh it never would do to let folks know
My sister's nothing but a great big crow.

TED HUGHES

The Older the Violin the Sweeter the Tune

Me Granny old
Me Granny wise
stories shine like a moon
from inside she eyes.

Me Granny can dance
Me Granny can sing
but she can't play the violin.

Yet she always saying,
"Dih older dih violin
de sweeter de tune."

Me Granny must be wiser
than the man inside the moon.

JOHN AGARD

For Nkemdilim, My Daughter

Nkemdilim, Nkemdilim,
run to me!
Do not stand there
making your cheeks swell out
like two big red tomatoes.
Do not push out your lips
like two red cherries
making figure eight.
Do not turn in your toes
like a duck,
making letter O

Nkemdilim – oo!
run to me, I say,
before I make your bottom red too
like the ripe tomatoes
of your sulky face!

IFI AMADIUME

Antigonish

As I was going up the stair
I met a man who wasn't there;
He wasn't there again today –
I wish, I wish he'd stay away.

HUGHES MEARNS

The King's Breakfast

The King asked
The Queen, and
The Queen asked
The Dairymaid:
"Could we have some butter for
The Royal slice of bread?"
The Queen asked
The Dairymaid,
The Dairymaid
Said, "Certainly,
I'll go and tell
The cow
Now
Before she goes to bed."

The Dairymaid
She curtsied,
And went and told
The Alderney:
"Don't forget the butter for
The Royal slice of bread."
The Alderney
Said sleepily:
"You'd better tell
His Majesty
That many people nowadays
Like marmalade
Instead."

The Dairymaid
Said, "Fancy!"
And went to
Her Majesty.
She curtsied to the Queen, and
She turned a little red:
"Excuse me,
Your Majesty,
For taking of
The liberty,
But marmalade is tasty, if
It's very
Thickly
Spread."

The Queen said
"Oh!"
And went to
His Majesty:
"Talking of the butter for
The royal slice of bread,
Many people
Think that
Marmalade
Is nicer.
Would you like to try a little
Marmalade
Instead?"

❁ ❁ ❁

The King said,
"Bother!"
And then he said,
"Oh, deary me!"
The King sobbed, "Oh, deary me!"
And went back to bed.
"Nobody,"
He whimpered,
"Could call me
A fussy man;
I *only* want
A little bit
Of butter for
My bread!"

❁ ❁ ❁

The Queen said,
"There, there!"
And went to
The Dairymaid.
The Dairymaid
Said, "There, there!"
And went to the shed.
The cow said,
"There, there!
I didn't really
Mean it;
Here's milk for his porringer
And butter for his bread."

❁ ❁ ❁

The Queen took
The butter
And brought it to
His Majesty;
The King said,
"Butter, eh?"
And bounced out of bed.
"Nobody," he said,
As he kissed her
Tenderly,
"Nobody," he said,
As he slid down
The banisters,
"Nobody,
My darling,
Could call me
A fussy man –
BUT
I do like a little bit of butter to my bread!"

❁ ❁ ❁

A. A. MILNE

❁ ❁ ❁

Visiting Mrs Neverley

Old Mrs Neverley
came from Back There.
She sat in the sunshine
with frost in her hair.
I'll be going home soon, she said.
Never said where.

Sweet crumbly biscuits,
ghostly-grey tea
and her smile would be waiting.
She listened to me
and sometimes to someone else
I couldn't see

and when we fell silent
and couldn't say why
she glanced at the window.
She smiled at the sky.
Look! There, you missed it.
An angel passed by.

It was one of her stories.
She said, *I'm growing too.*
You grow up, I grow down.
She told lies, I knew.
Only, now that she's gone
nothing else quite seems true.

PHILIP GROSS

Over Land and Sea

The Child in the Train

The train stands still
  And the world runs by.
Yonder runs a tree
  And a cloud in the sky.
Here flies a pony
  On the running road,
And there flows the quickest
  River ever flowed.

The mountains on the edge
  Roll away like the tide,
The backs of the houses,
  Pass on a slide,
The little farms slip off
  As soon as one looks,
And the little churches vanish
  With their spires and their rooks.

The buttercup embankments,
  The telegraph wires,
The names of the stations,
  The small heath fires,
The hoardings in the fields,
  And the people in the street,
Go whizzing into somewhere
  While I keep my seat.

The little cities trot,
  And the little hamlets trip,
The meadow with its cow,
  The sea with its ship,
The forest and the factory,
  The hedge and the hill –
The world goes running by
  While the train stands still!

ELEANOR FARJEON

The Green Train

The Blue Train for the South – but the Green Train for us.
Nobody knows when the Green Train departs.
Nobody sees her off. There is no noise; no fuss;
No luggage on the Green Train;
No whistle when she starts.
But quietly at the right time they wave the green light
And she slides past the platform and plunges into the night.

Wonderful people walking down the long Green Train,
As the engine gathers speed.
And voices talking.
"Where does she go to, Guard?"
Where indeed?
But what does it matter
So long as the night is starred?
Who cares for time, and who cares for place,
So long as the Green Train thunders on into space?

E.V. RIEU

From a Railway Carriage

Faster than fairies, faster than witches,
Bridges and houses, hedges and ditches;
And charging along like troops in a battle,
All through the meadows the horses and cattle:
All of the sights of the hill and the plain
Fly as thick as driving rain;
And ever again, in the wink of an eye,
Painted stations whistle by.

Here is a child who clambers and scrambles,
All by himself and gathering brambles;
Here is a tramp who stands and gazes;
And there is the green for stringing the daisies!
Here is a cart run away in the road
Lumping along with man and load;
And here is a mill and there is a river:
Each a glimpse and gone for ever!

ROBERT LOUIS STEVENSON

Adlestrop

Yes. I remember Adlestrop –
The name, because one afternoon
Of heat the express-train drew up there
Unwontedly. It was late June.

The steam hissed. Someone cleared his throat.
No one left and no one came
On the bare platform. What I saw
Was Adlestrop – only the name

And willows, willow-herb, and grass,
And meadowsweet, and haycocks dry,
No whit less still and lonely fair
Than the high cloudlets in the sky.

And for that minute a blackbird sang
Close by, and round him, mistier,
Farther and farther, all the birds
Of Oxfordshire and Gloucestershire.

EDWARD THOMAS

Where Go the Boats?

Dark brown is the river,
Golden is the sand.
It flows along for ever,
With trees on either hand.

Green leaves a-floating,
Castles of the foam,
Boats of mine a-boating –
Where will all come home?

On goes the river
And out past the mill,
Away down the valley,
Away down the hill.

Away down the river,
A hundred miles or more,
Other little children
Shall bring my boats ashore.

ROBERT LOUIS STEVENSON

Roadways

One road leads to London,
One road runs to Wales,
My road leads me seawards
To the white dipping sails.

One road leads to the river,
As it goes singing slow;
My road leads to shipping,
Where the bronzed sailors go.

Leads me, lures me, calls me
To salt, green, tossing sea;
A road without earth's road-dust
Is the right road for me.

A wet road, heaving, shining,
   And wild with seagulls' cries,
A mad salt sea-wind blowing
   The salt spray in my eyes.

My road calls me, lures me
   West, east, south, and north;
Most roads lead men homewards,
   My road leads me forth.

To add more miles to the tally
   Of grey miles left behind,
In quest of that one beauty
   God put me here to find.

JOHN MASEFIELD

Morwenstow

Where do you come from, sea,
To the sharp Cornish shore,
Leaping up to the raven's crag?
      From Labrador.

Do you grow tired, sea?
Are you weary ever
When the storms burst over your head?
      Never.

Are you hard as a diamond, sea,
As iron, as oak?
Are you stronger than flint or steel?
      And the lightning stroke.

Ten thousand years and more, sea,
You have gobbled your fill,
Swallowing stone and slate!
      I am hungry still.

When will you rest, sea?
   When moon and sun
   Ride only fields of salt water
   And the land is gone.

CHARLES CAUSLEY

Grim and Gloomy

Oh, grim and gloomy,
So grim and gloomy
Are the caves beneath the sea.
Oh, rare but roomy
And bare and boomy,
Those salt sea caverns be.

Oh, slim and slimy
Or grey and grimy
Are the animals of the sea.
Salt and oozy
And safe and snoozy
The caves where those animals be.

Hark to the shuffling,
Huge and snuffling,
Ravenous, cavernous, great sea-beasts!
But fair and fabulous,
Tintinnabulous,
Gay and fabulous are their feasts.

Ah, but the queen of the sea,
The querulous, perilous sea!
How the curls of her tresses
The pearls on her dresses,
Sway and swirl in the waves,
How cosy and dozy,
How sweet ring-a-rosy
Her bower in the deep-sea caves!

Oh, rare but roomy
And bare and boomy
Those caverns under the sea,
And grave and grandiose,
Safe and sandiose
The dens of her denizens be.

JAMES REEVES

Sing Something Simple

Oh! Dear!

Oh! dear! what can the matter be?
Dear! dear! what can the matter be?
Oh! dear! what can the matter be?
Johnny's so long at the fair.

He promised he'd buy me a fairing should please me,
And then for a kiss, oh! he vowed he would tease me,
He promised he'd bring me a bunch of blue ribbons
To tie up my bonny brown hair.

And it's oh! dear! what can the matter be?
Dear! dear! what can the matter be?
Oh! dear! what can the matter be?
Johnny's so long at the fair.

He promised he'd bring me a basket of posies,
A garland of lilies, a garland of roses,
A little straw hat, to set off the blue ribbons
That tie up my bonny brown hair.

And it's oh! dear! what can the matter be?
Dear! dear! what can the matter be?
Oh! dear! what can the matter be?
Johnny's so long at the fair.

TRADITIONAL

The Milkmaid

Where are you going to, my pretty maid?
I'm going a-milking, sir, she said,
Sir, she said, sir, she said,
I'm going a-milking, sir, she said.

May I go with you, my pretty maid?
You're kindly welcome, sir, she said,
Sir, she said, sir, she said,
You're kindly welcome, sir, she said.

Say, will you marry me, my pretty maid?
Yes, if you please, kind sir, she said,
Sir, she said, sir, she said,
Yes, if you please, kind sir, she said.

What is your father, my pretty maid?
My father's a farmer, sir, she said,
Sir, she said, sir, she said,
My father's a farmer, sir, she said.

What is your fortune, my pretty maid?
My face is my fortune, sir, she said,
Sir, she said, sir, she said,
My face is my fortune, sir, she said.

Then I can't marry you, my pretty maid.
Nobody asked you, sir, she said,
Sir, she said, sir, she said,
Nobody asked you, sir, she said.

ANON

Soldier, Soldier, Will You Marry Me?

Oh, soldier, soldier, will you marry me,
With your musket, fife and drum?
Oh no, pretty maid, I cannot marry you,
For I have no coat to put on.

Then away she went to the tailor's shop
As fast as legs could run,
And bought him one of the very very best,
And the soldier put it on.

Oh, soldier, soldier, will you marry me,
With your musket, fife, and drum?
Oh no, pretty maid, I cannot marry you,
For I have no shoes to put on.

Then away she went to the cobbler's shop
As fast as legs could run,
And bought him a pair of the very very best,
And the soldier put them on.

Oh, soldier, soldier, will you marry me,
With your musket, fife and drum?
Oh no, pretty maid, I cannot marry you,
For I have a wife at home.

TRADITIONAL

The Little Man and Maid

There was a little man
And he woo'd a little maid,
And he said, "Little maid, will you wed, wed, wed?
I have little more to say
Than 'will you, yea or nay?'
For least said is soonest mended-ded-ded-ded."

The little maid replied,
(Some say a little sighed),
"But what shall we have to eat, eat, eat?
Will the love that you are rich in
Make a fire in the kitchen?
Or the little god of loving turn the spit, spit, spit?"

TRADITIONAL

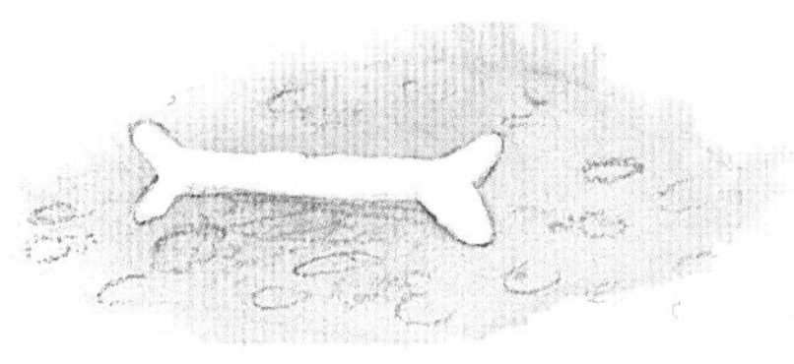

Lavender's Blue

Lavender's blue, dilly dilly, lavender's green,
When I am king, dilly dilly, you shall be queen
Who told you so, dilly dilly, who told you so?
'Twas mine own heart, dilly dilly, that told me so.

Call up your men, dilly dilly, set them to work,
Some with a rake, dilly dilly, some with a fork,
Some to make hay, dilly dilly, some to thresh corn,
Whilst you and I, dilly dilly, keep ourselves warm.

TRADITIONAL

The Jolly Miller

There was a jolly miller once
Lived on the river Dee;
He worked and sang from morn till night,
No lark more blithe than he.
And this the burden of his song
Forever used to be,
"I care for nobody, no, not I,
And nobody cares for me!"

TRADITIONAL

Song for a Banjo Dance

Shake your brown feet, honey,
Shake your brown feet, chile,
Shake your brown feet, honey,
Shake 'em swift and wil'–
        Get way back, honey,
        Do that rockin' step.
        Slide on over, darling,
                Now! Come out
                With your left.
Shake your brown feet, honey,
Shake 'em, honey chile.

Sun's going down this evening –
Might never rise no mo'.
The sun's going down this very night –
Might never rise no mo'
So dance with swift feet, honey,
        (The banjo's sobbing low)
Dance with swift feet, honey –
        Might never dance no mo'.

Shake your brown feet, Liza,
Shake 'em, Liza, chile,
Shake your brown feet, Liza,
        (The music's soft and wil')
Shake your brown feet, Liza,
        (The banjo's sobbing low)
The sun's going down this very night –
Might never rise no mo'.

LANGSTON HUGHES

Song Sung by a Man on a Barge to Another Man on a Different Barge in Order to Drive Him Mad

Oh,

I am the best bargee bar none,
You are the best bargee bar one!
You are the second-best bargee,
You are the best bargee bar me!

Oh,

I am the best......

(and so on, until he is
hurled into the canal)

KIT WRIGHT

Rope Rhyme

Get set, ready now, jump right in
Bounce and kick and giggle and spin
Listen to the rope when it hits the ground
Listen to that clappedy-slappedy sound
Jump right up when it tells you to
Come back down whatever you do
Count to a hundred, count by ten
Start to count all over again
That's what jumping is all about
Get set, ready now,
jump
right
out!

ELOISE GREENFIELD

Captain Cat's Song

Johnnie Crack and Flossie Snail
Kept their baby in a milking pail
Flossie Snail and Johnnie Crack
One would pull it out and one would put it back

O it's my turn now said Flossie Snail
To take the baby from the milking pail
And it's my turn now said Johnnie Crack
To smack it on the head and put it back

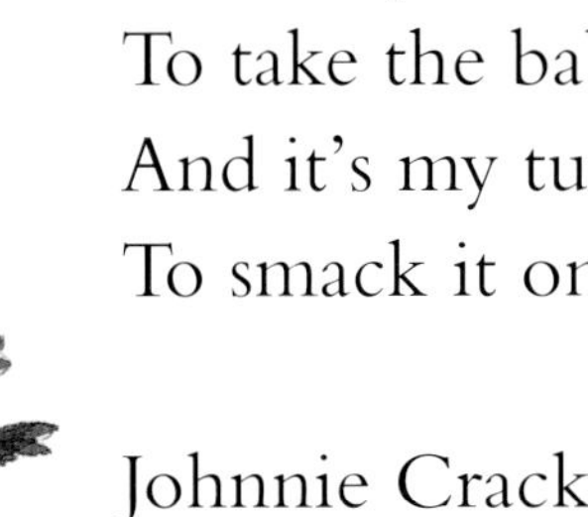

Johnnie Crack and Flossie Snail
Kept their baby in a milking pail
One would put it back and one would pull it out
And all it had to drink was ale and stout
For Johnnie Crack and Flossie Snail
Always used to say that stout and ale
Was *good* for a baby in a milking pail.

DYLAN THOMAS

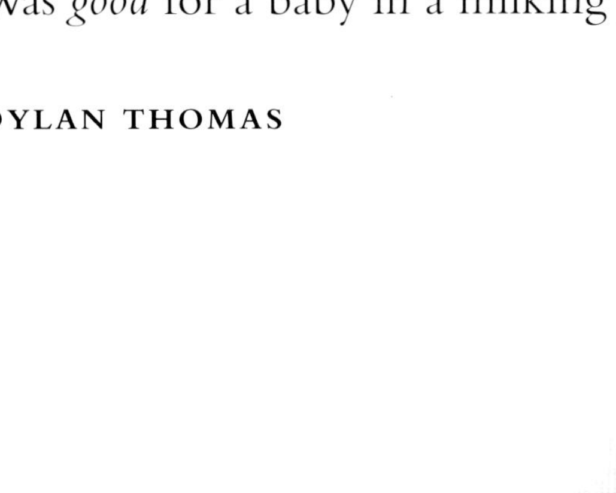

The Bells of London

Gay go up and gay go down,
To ring the bells of London town.
Halfpence and farthings,
Say the bells of St Martin's.
Oranges and lemons,
Say the bells of St Clement's.
Pancakes and fritters,
Say the bells of St Peter's.
Two sticks and an apple,
Say the bells of Whitechapel.

Kettles and pans,
Say the bells of St Ann's.
You owe me ten shillings,
Say the bells of St Helen's.
When will you pay me?
Say the bells of Old Bailey.
When I grow rich,
Say the bells of Shoreditch.
Pray when will that be?
Say the bells of Stepney.
I am sure I don't know,
Says the great bell of Bow.

TRADITIONAL

I Had a Little Nut Tree

I had a little nut tree,
Nothing would it bear,
But a silver nutmeg,
And a golden pear.
The King of Spain's daughter
Came to visit me,
And all was because of
My little nut tree.
I skipped over water
I danced over sea,
And all the birds in the air
Could not catch me.

ANON

The Death and Burial of Cock Robin

Who killed Cock Robin?
  I, said the Sparrow,
  With my bow and arrow,
I killed Cock Robin.

Who saw him die?
  I, said the Fly,
  With my little eye,
I saw him die.

Who caught his blood?
  I, said the Fish,
  With my little dish,
I caught his blood.

Who'll make his shroud?
  I, said the Beetle,
  With my thread and needle,
I'll make his shroud.

Who'll dig his grave?
  I, said the Owl,
  With my pick and shovel,
I'll dig his grave.

Who'll be the parson?
  I, said the Rook,
  With my little book,
I'll be the parson.

Who'll be the clerk?
  I, said the Lark,
  If it's not in the dark,
I'll be the clerk.

Who'll bear the pall?
  We, said the Wren,
  Both the cock and the hen,
We'll bear the pall.

Who'll carry the link?
  I, said the Linnet,
  I'll fetch it in a minute,
I'll carry the link.

Who'll be the chief mourner?
  I, said the Dove,
  I mourn for my love,
I'll be chief mourner.

Who'll carry the coffin?
  I, said the Kite,
  If it's not through the night,
I'll carry the coffin.

Who'll sing the psalm?
  I, said the Thrush,
  As she sat on a bush,
I'll sing a psalm.

Who'll toll the bell?
  I, said the Bull,
  Because I can pull,
So Cock Robin, farewell.

All the birds of the air
  Fell a–sighing and a–sobbing,
  When they heard the bell toll
For poor Cock Robin.

TRADITIONAL

Leaves

Who's killed the leaves?
Me, says the apple, I've killed them all.
Fat as a bomb or a cannonball
I've killed the leaves.

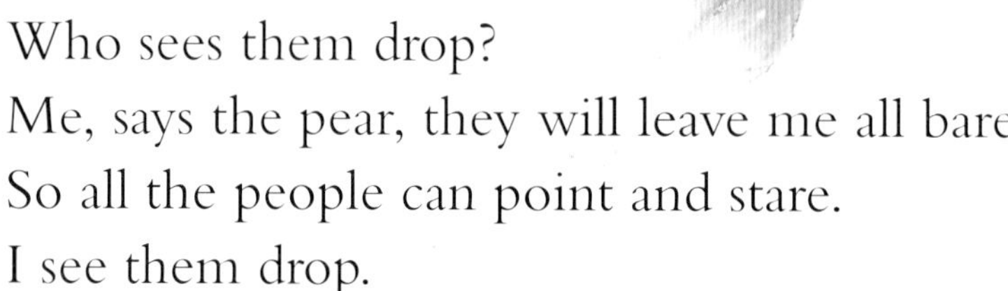

Who sees them drop?
Me, says the pear, they will leave me all bare
So all the people can point and stare.
I see them drop.

Who'll catch their blood?
Me, me, me, says the marrow, the marrow.
I'll get so rotund that they'll need a wheelbarrow.
I'll catch their blood.

Who'll make their shroud?
Me, says the swallow, there's just time enough
Before I must pack all my spools and be off.
I'll make their shroud.

Who'll dig their grave?
Me, says the river, with the power of the clouds
A brown deep grave I'll dig under my floods.
I'll dig their grave.

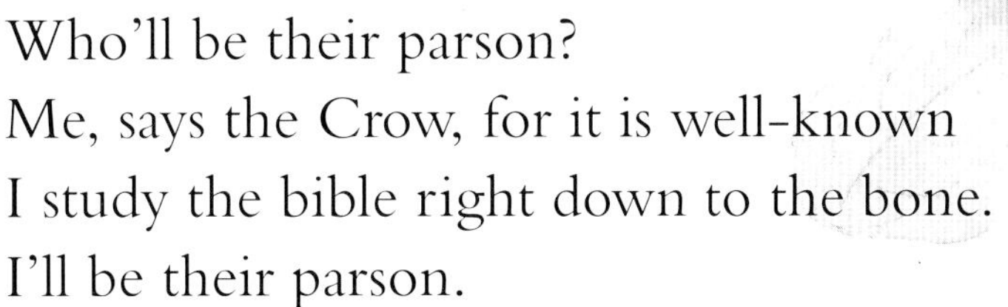

Who'll be their parson?
Me, says the Crow, for it is well-known
I study the bible right down to the bone.
I'll be their parson.

Who'll be chief mourner?
Me, says the wind, I will cry through the grass
The people will pale and go cold when I pass.
I'll be chief mourner.

Who'll carry the coffin?
Me, says the sunset, the whole world will weep
To see me lower it into the deep.
I'll carry the coffin.

Who'll sing a psalm?
Me, says the tractor, with my gear grinding glottle
I'll plough up the stubble and sing through my throttle.
I'll sing the psalm.

Who'll toll the bell?
Me, says the robin, my song in October
Will tell the still gardens the leaves are over.
I'll toll the bell.

TED HUGHES

Mean Song

Snickles and podes,
Ribble and grodes:
That's what I wish you.

A nox in the groot,
A root in the stoot
And a gock in the forbeshaw, too.

Keep out of sight
For fear that I might
Glom you a gravely snave.

Don't show your face
Around any place
Or you'll get one flack snack in the bave.

EVE MERRIAM

Who's Out There?

The Frozen Man

Out at the edge of town
where black trees

crack their fingers
in the icy wind

and hedges freeze
on their shadows

and the breath of cattle,
still as boulders,

hangs in rags
under the rolling moon,

a man is walking
alone:

on the coal-black road
his cold

feet
ring

and
ring.

Here in a snug house
at the heart of town

the fire is burning
red and yellow and gold:

you can hear the warmth
like a sleeping cat

breathe softly
in every room.

When the frozen man
comes to the door,

let him in,
let him in,
let him in.

KIT WRIGHT

Some One

Some one came knocking
At my wee, small door;
Some one came knocking,
I'm sure – sure – sure;
I listened, I opened,
I looked to left and right,
But nought there was a-stirring
In the still dark night;
Only the busy beetle
Tap-tapping in the wall,
Only from the forest
The screech-owl's call,
Only the cricket whistling
While the dewdrops fall,
So I know not who came knocking,
At all, at all, at all.

WALTER DE LA MARE

The Sound Collector

A stranger called this morning
Dressed all in black and grey
Put every sound into a bag
And carried them away

The whistling of the kettle
The turning of the lock
The purring of the kitten
The ticking of the clock

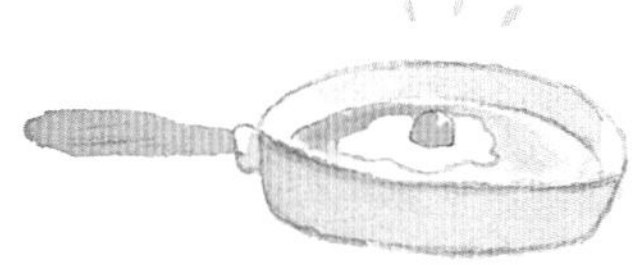

The popping of the toaster
The crunching of the flakes
When you spread the marmalade
The scraping noise it makes

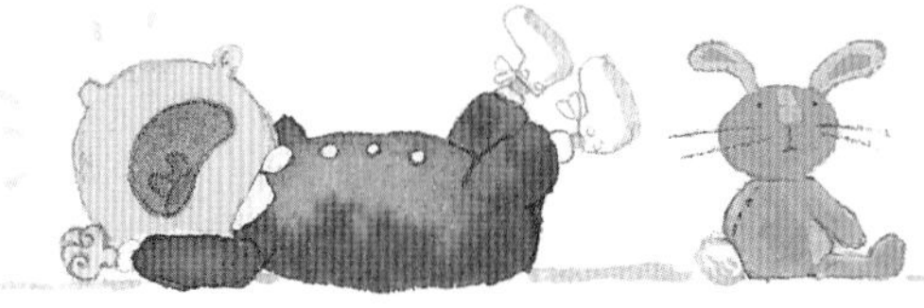

The hissing of the frying-pan
The ticking of the grill
The bubbling of the bathtub
As it starts to fill

The drumming of the raindrops
On the window-pane
When you do the washing-up
The gurgle of the drain

The crying of the baby
The squeaking of the chair
The swishing of the curtain
The creaking of the stair

A stranger called this morning
He didn't leave his name
Left us only silence
Life will never be the same.

ROGER McGOUGH

Windy Nights

Whenever the moon and stars are set,
  Whenever the wind is high,
All night long in the dark and wet,
  A man goes riding by.
Late in the night when the fires are out,
Why does he gallop and gallop about?

Whenever the trees are crying aloud,
  And ships are tossed at sea,
By, on the highway, low and loud,
  By at the gallop goes he.
By at the gallop he goes, and then
By he comes back at the gallop again.

ROBERT LOUIS STEVENSON

Golden Days, Silver Nights

A Valentine Poem for Cathy Pompe's Kids at St Paul's Primary School, Cambridge (*who were about 6-7 years old*)

The night is a dark blue balloon
The day is a golden balloon
The moon longs to cuddle the sun
The sun longs to cuddle the moon

ADRIAN MITCHELL

The Early Morning

The moon on the one hand, the dawn on the other:
The moon is my sister, the dawn is my brother.
The moon on my left and the dawn on my right.
My brother, good morning: my sister, good night.

HILAIRE BELLOC

The Sun's Travels

The sun is not a-bed, when I
At night upon my pillow lie;
Still round the earth his way he takes,
And morning after morning makes.

While here at home, in shining day,
We round the sunny garden play,
Each little Indian sleepy-head
Is being kissed and put to bed.

And when at eve I rise from tea,
Day dawns beyond the Atlantic Sea;
And all the children in the West
Are getting up and being dressed.

ROBERT LOUIS STEVENSON

Is the Moon Tired?

Is the moon tired? She looks so pale
Within her misty veil;
She scales the sky from east to west,
And takes no rest.

Before the coming of the night
The moon shows papery white;
Before the dawning of the day,
She fades away.

CHRISTINA ROSSETTI

Early Country Village Morning

Cocks crowing
Hens knowing
later they will cluck
their laying song

Houses stirring
a donkey clip-clopping
the first market bus
comes jugging along

Soon the sun will give a big yawn
and open her eye
pushing the last bit of darkness
out of the sky

GRACE NICHOLS

Flying

I saw the moon,
One windy night,
Flying so fast –
All silvery white –
Over the sky
Like a toy balloon
Loose from its string –
A runaway moon.
The frosty stars
Went racing past,
Chasing her on
Ever so fast.
Then everyone said,
"It's the clouds that fly,
And the stars and moon
Stand still in the sky."
But I don't mind –
I saw the moon
Sailing away
Like a toy
Balloon.

J.M. WESTRUP

Silver

Slowly, silently, now the moon
Walks the night in her silver shoon;
This way, and that, she peers, and sees
Silver fruit upon silver trees;
One by one the casements catch
Her beams beneath the silvery thatch;
Couched in his kennel, like a log,
With paws of silver sleeps the dog;
From their shadowy cote the white breasts peep
Of doves in a silver-feathered sleep;
A harvest mouse goes scampering by,
With silver claws, and silver eye;
And moveless fish in the water gleam,
By silver reeds in a silver stream.

WALTER DE LA MARE

Night Sounds

When I lie in bed
I think I can hear
The stars being switched on
I think I can.

And I think I can hear
The moon
Breathing.

But I have to be still.
So still.
All the house is sleeping.
Except for me.

Then I think I can hear it.

BERLIE DOHERTY

Waking at Night

What has happened? Is this me?
Who am I? Where can I be?
Where's the fireplace? Where's the door?
I can't remember any more.

If I'm me, the rocking-chair
Should be in the window there,
But the window's turned around
In the dark, and can't be found.

Strange that though the room is dark
I just know it's twisted. Hark!
That's the cuckoo-clock – how queer! –
Ticking there instead of here.

Something's happened to my bed,
Head is foot and foot is head,
And the wall has shifted quite
From my left side to my right.

Then this room is *not* the one
I know – it has come undone,
Window, fireplace, door and wall,
And I can't be me at all!

ELEANOR FARJEON

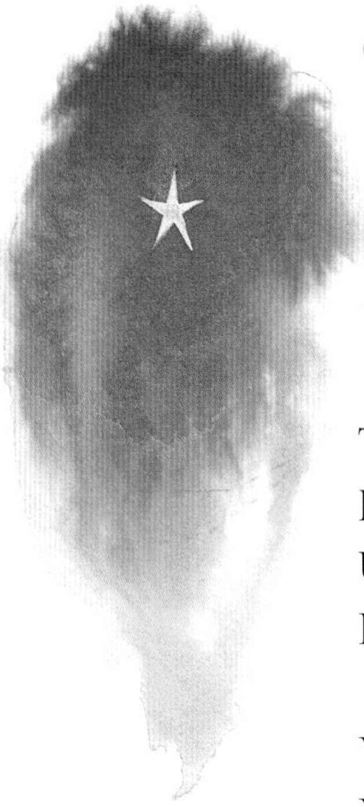

The Star

Twinkle, twinkle, little star,
How I wonder what you are!
Up above the world so high,
Like a diamond in the sky.

When the blazing sun is gone,
When he nothing shines upon,
Then you show your little light,
Twinkle, twinkle, all the night.

Then the traveller in the dark,
Thanks you for your tiny spark,
He could not see which way to go,
If you did not twinkle so.

In the dark blue sky you keep,
And often through my curtains peep,
For you never shut your eye,
Till the sun is in the sky.

As your bright and tiny spark,
Lights the traveller in the dark –
Though I know not what you are,
Twinkle, twinkle, little star.

JANE TAYLOR

♥ REFLECTIONS ♥

Our Hamster's Life

Our hamster's life:
there's not much
to it,
not much
to it.

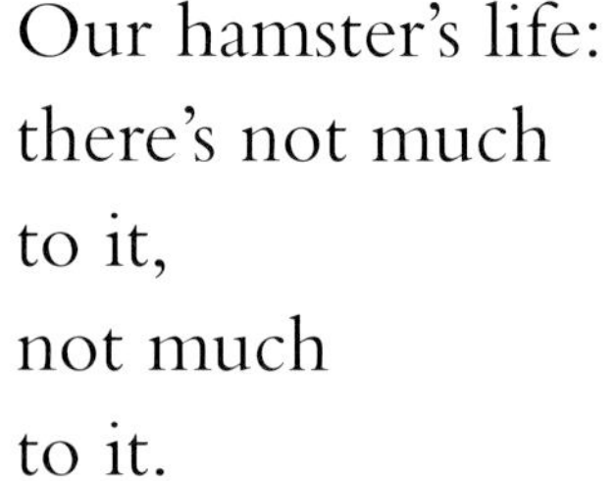
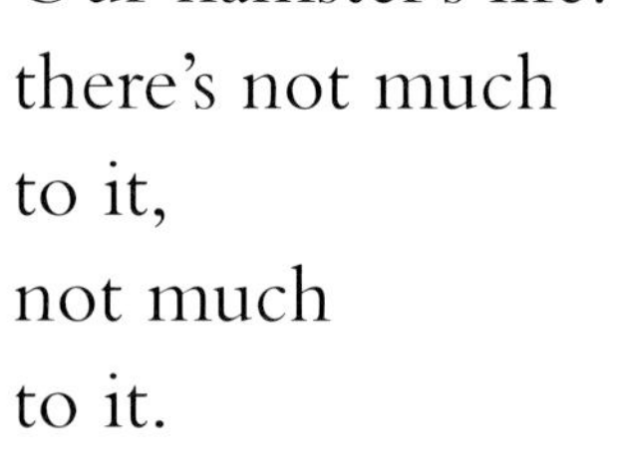

He presses his pink nose
to the door of his cage
and decides for the fifty six
millionth time
that he can't get
through it.

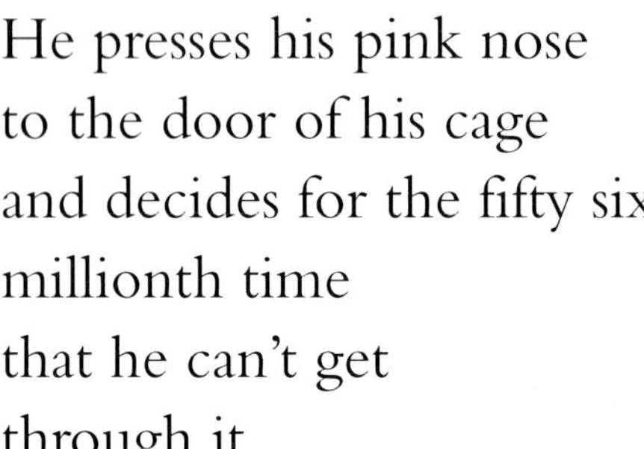

Our hamster's life:
there's not much
to it,
not much
to it.

It's about the most boring
life in the world,
if he only
knew it.
He sleeps and he drinks and he eats.
He eats and he drinks and he sleeps.

He slinks and he dreeps.
He eats.

This process
he repeats.

Our hamster's life:
there's not much
to it,
not much
to it.

You'd think it would drive him bonkers,
going round and round on his wheel.
It's certainly driving me bonkers,

watching him
do it.

But he may be thinking:
"That boy's life,
there's not much
to it,
not much
to it:

watching a hamster go round on a wheel,
It's driving me bonkers if he only knew it,

watching him
watching me
do it."

KIT WRIGHT

Busy Day

Pop in
pop out
pop over the road
pop out for a walk
pop in for a talk
pop down to the shop
can't stop
got to pop

got to pop?

pop where?
pop what?

well
I've got to
pop round
pop up
pop in to town
pop out and see
pop in for tea
pop down to the shop
can't stop
got to pop

got to pop?

pop where?
pop what?

well
I've got to
pop in
pop out
pop over the road
pop out for a walk
pop in for a talk........

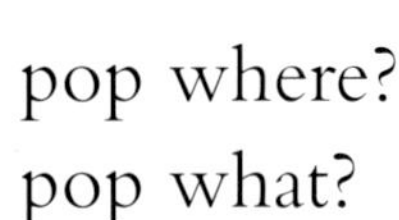

MICHAEL ROSEN

Scowling

When I see you
scowling

I want to turn you
upside down

and see you
smile!

ROGER McGOUGH

Youth and Age

Impatient of his childhood,
"Ah me!" exclaimed young Arthur,
Whilst roving in the wild wood,
"I wish I were my father!"
Meanwhile, to see his Arthur
So skip, and play, and run,
"Ah me!" exclaims the father,
"I wish I were my son!"

THOMAS HOOD

Kind Deeds

Little drops of water,
Little grains of sand,
Make the mighty ocean,
And the pleasant land.

Thus the little minutes,
Humble though they be,
Make the mighty ages
Of eternity.

Little deeds of kindness,
Little words of love,
Make this earth an Eden
Like the heaven above.

ISAAC WATTS

Twenty-Six Letters

Twenty-six cards in half a pack;
Twenty-six weeks in half a year;
Twenty-six letters dressed in black
In all the words you ever will hear.

In 'King', 'Queen', 'Ace', and 'Jack',
In 'London', 'lucky', 'lone', and 'lack',
'January', 'April', 'fortify', 'fix',
You'll never find more than twenty-six.

Think of the beautiful things you see
On mountain, riverside, meadow and tree.
How many their names are, but how small
The twenty-six letters that spell them all.

JAMES REEVES

Shallow Poem

I've thought of a poem.
I carry it carefully,
nervously, in my head,
like a saucer of milk;
in case I should spill some lines
before I can put it down.

GERDA MAYER

Bluebells and Penguins

The day we found the lady
Crying in the wood
We tried to comfort her
As best we could
But just what she was crying for
We never understood:

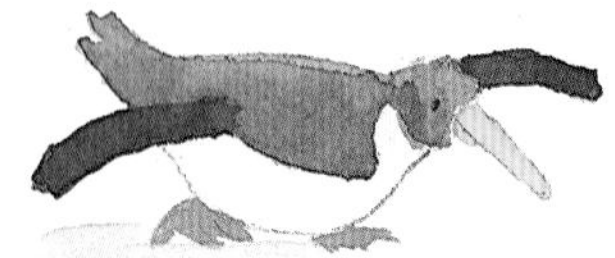

Weeping among the beechleaves and the bluebells.

The day we saw the old man
Cackling at the zoo
We had a laugh along with him
The way you do
But just what he was laughing at
We never had a clue:

Chuckling among the pythons and the penguins!

Now penguins aren't that funny
And bluebells aren't that sad
But sometimes you feel really good
And sometimes you feel bad.
Sometimes you feel sky-high happy,
Sometimes lost and low,
And why on earth you feel like that
Sometimes
you
don't
know!

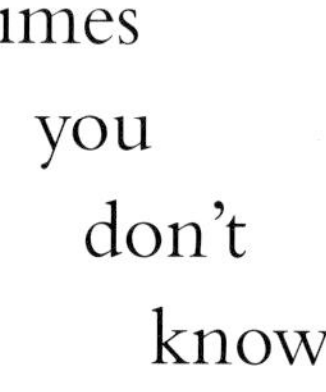

KIT WRIGHT

Leisure

What is this life if, full of care,
We have no time to stand and stare?

No time to stand beneath the boughs
And stare as long as sheep or cows.

No time to see, when woods we pass,
Where squirrels hide their nuts in grass.

No time to see, in broad daylight,
Streams full of stars, like skies at night.

No time to turn at Beauty's glance,
And watch her feet, how they can dance.

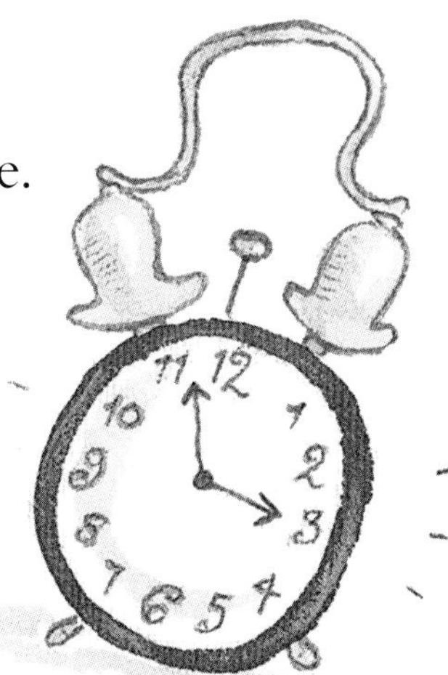

No time to wait till her mouth can
Enrich that smile her eyes began.

A poor life this if, full of care,
We have no time to stand and stare.

W.H. DAVIES

If all the Seas Were one Sea

If all the seas were one sea,
What a *great* sea that would be!
If all the trees were one tree,
What a *great* tree that would be!
And if all the axes were one axe,
What a *great* axe that would be!
And if all the men were one man,
What a *great* man that would be!
And if the *great* man took the *great* axe,
And cut down the *great* tree,
And let it fall into the *great* sea,
What a splish-splash that would be!

ANON

Fortunes

One for sorrow, two for joy,
Three for a kiss and four for a boy,
Five for silver, six for gold,
Seven for a secret never to be told,
Eight for a letter from over the sea,
Nine for a lover as true as can be.

TRADITIONAL

Solomon Grundy

Solomon Grundy,
Born on a Monday,
Christened on Tuesday,
Married on Wednesday,
Took ill on Thursday,
Worse on Friday,
Died on Saturday,
Buried on Sunday.
This is the end
Of Solomon Grundy.

ANON

Star Light, Star Bright...

Star light, star bright,
First star I've seen tonight,
Wish I may, wish I might,
Have this wish I wish tonight.

ANON

I am a Gold Lock

(Ask a friend to repeat each line after you)

I am a gold lock.
I am a gold key.

I am a silver lock.
I am a silver key.

I am a brass lock.
I am a brass key.

I am a lead lock.
I am a lead key.

I am a monk lock.
I am a monk key!

TRADITIONAL

INDEX OF TITLES AND FIRST LINES

Titles are in *italics.* Where the title and the first line are the same, the first line only is listed.

INDEX OF AUTHORS

ACKNOWLEDGEMENTS

The publisher would like to thank the copyright holders for permission to reproduce the following copyright material. Every effort has been made to trace the ownership of all copyrighted material and to secure the necessary permission to reprint these selections. In the event of any question arising as to the use of any material, the editor and publisher, while expressing regret for any inadvertent error, will be happy to make the necessary correction in future printings.

• John Agard: 'Cat in the Dark' from *I Din Do Nothing* (The Bodley Head, 1983); 'The Older the Violin, the Sweeter the Tune' from *Say it again Granny* (The Bodley Head). Reprinted by permission of Random Century Ltd. • Ifi Amadiume: 'For Nkemdilim, my daughter' from *Passion Waves* (Karnak House, 1985). Reprinted by permission of Karnak House. • Hilaire Belloc: 'The Elephant' and 'The Early Morning' from *Complete Verse* (Pimlico, a division of Random Century). Reprinted by permission of the Peters Fraser & Dunlop Group Ltd. • Charles Causley: 'Morwenstow' from *Jack the Treacle-Eater* (Macmillan, 1987), 'Spin me a web, spider' from *Early in the Morning* (Penguin, 1986). Reprinted by permission of David Higham Associates. • Stanley Cook: 'Colouring', 'Chips' and 'In the Street' from *Dragon on the Wall* by Stanley Cook, copyright © 1989. First published by Blackie & Son. • E. E. Cummings: 'little tree' is reprinted from *Complete Poems 1904-1962*, by E. E. Cummings, edited by George J. Firmage, by permission of W. W. Norton & Company Ltd. Copyright © 1925, 1953, 1976, 1991 by the Trustees for the E. E. Cummings Trust and George James Firmage. • John Cunliffe: 'Cat Warmth' from *Standing on a Strawberry* (André Deutsch, 1987). Reprinted by permission of Scholastic Publications Ltd. • Walter de la Mare: 'Silver', 'Snow', 'Some one' and 'The Window' reprinted by permission of The Literary Trustees of Walter de la Mare, and the Society of Authors as their representative. • Berlie Doherty: 'Night Sounds' from *Walking on Air* (HarperCollins Publishers Ltd, 1993). Reprinted by permission of Murray Pollinger. • Lord Alfred Douglas: 'The Shark' (Edward Arnold Ltd). Reprinted by permission of David Higham Associates. • Richard Edwards: 'Hide and Seek' reprinted by permission of Richard Edwards; 'To Pass the Time' from *Verse Universe*, ed John Tuckey, 1992, by permission of Orchard Books. • Gavin Ewart: 'Zebra' from *Learned Hippopotamus* by Gavin Ewart (Hutchinson) • Eleanor Farjeon: 'The Child in the Train' from *Something I Remember*, ed Anne Harvey (Blackie & Son, 1987), copyright © Gervase Farjeon, 1987; 'Cottage' from *Cherrystones* (Michael Joseph, 1942); 'Waking at Night' from *Invitation to a Mouse*, ed. Annabel Farjeon (Hodder & Stoughton), copyright © executors of Eleanor Farjeon, 1916-51 • Max Fatchen: 'Just When' from *Wry Rhymes for Troublesome Times* by Max Fatchen (published by Viking Kestrel and in Puffin books), copyright © Max Fatchen 1983; 'My Dog' from *Songs for My Dog and Other People* by Max Fatchen (published by Viking Kestrel and in Puffin Books), copyright © Max Fatchen, 1980. • Nikki Giovanni: 'sleep' and 'springtime' from *Spin a Soft Black Song* by Nikki Giovanni, copyright © Nikki Giovanni, 1971. Reprinted by permission of Farrar, Straus & Giroux, Inc. • Eloise Greenfield: 'Rope Rhyme' from *Honey I Love* (HarperCollins, 1978). Reprinted by permission of Marie Brown Associates. Copyright © Eloise Greenfield, 1978. • Philip Gross: 'Visiting Mrs Neverley' printed by permission of Philip Gross. • John Heath-Stubbs: 'The Blackbird' from *The Parliament of Birds* (Chatto & Windus). Reprinted by permission of David Higham Associates. • Langston Hughes: 'Song for a Banjo Dance' from *The Weary Blues* by Langston Hughes. Copyright © 1926 by Alfred A. Knopf, Inc. and renewed 1954 by Langston Hughes. Reprinted by permission of Alfred A. Knopf, Inc. and David Higham Associates. • Ted Hughes: 'Leaves' from *Season's Songs* (Faber and Faber Ltd, 1976), copyright © Ted Hughes, 1968, 1973, 1975. Used by permission of Faber and Faber Ltd and Viking Penguin, a division of Penguin Books USA Inc.; 'Moon-Transport' and 'Tree-Disease' from *Moon-Whales* (Faber and Faber Ltd, 1976/88), copyright © Ted Hughes 1963, 1976. Used by permission of Faber and Faber Ltd and Viking Penguin, a division of Penguin Books USA Inc.; 'My Sister Jane' from *Meet My Folks* (Faber and Faber Ltd); 'Cow', 'Squirrel' and 'Worm' from *The Cat and the Cuckoo* (Sunstone Press, 1987), reprinted by permission of Ted Hughes. • Margaret Mahy: 'The Man from the Land of Fandango' from *Nonstop Nonsense*, reprinted with the permission of the publishers J. M. Dent and Margaret K. McElderry Books, an imprint of Macmillan Publishing Company. Copyright © Margaret Mahy, 1977. • John Masefield: 'Roadways' from *Collected Poems* (Heinemann, 1923, 1946, 1961) reprinted by permission of The Society of Authors as the literary representative of the Estate of John Masefield. • Gerda Mayer: 'Shallow Poem' from *Ambit*, 1971 and *The Knockabout Show* by Gerda Mayer (Chatto & Windus, 1978), copyright © Gerda Mayer, 1971. • Roger McGough: 'Scowling' and 'The Sound Collector' from *Pillow Talk* (Viking, 1990). Reprinted by permission of the Peters Fraser & Dunlop Group Ltd. • Irene McLeod: 'Lone Dog' from *Songs to Save a Soul* (Chatto & Windus) reprinted by permission of the Estate of Irene Rutherford McLeod. • A. A. Milne: 'The Little Black Hen' from *Now We Are Six* (Methuen, 1927), copyright © E. P. Dutton, 1927, renewed copyright © by A. A. Milne, 1955. Used by permission of Reed Book Services and Dutton Children's Books, a division of Penguin Books USA Inc.; 'The King's Breakfast' from *When We Were Very Young* (Methuen, 1924), copyright © 1924 by E. P. Dutton, renewed © by A. A. Milne, 1952. Used by permission of Reed Book Services and Dutton Children's Books, a division of Penguin Books USA Inc. • Adrian Mitchell: 'Not a Very Cheerful Song, I'm Afraid' and 'A Valentine Poem for Cathy Pompe's Kids at St Paul's Primary School, Cambridge' from *Nothingmas Day* (Allison & Busby, 1984). Reprinted with the permission of the Peters Fraser & Dunlop Group Ltd; 'Mrs Christmas' from *All My Own Stuff* (Simon & Schuster Young Books, 1984-91). Reproduced by permission of Simon & Schuster Young Books, Hemel Hempstead, UK. None of Adrian Mitchell's poems are to be used in connection with any examination whatsoever. • John Mole: 'The Waiting Game' from *Catching the Spider* by John Mole, copyright © John Mole, 1990. First published by Blackie Children's Books. • Grace Nichols: 'Come on into my tropical garden', 'Country Village Morning', and 'I am the Rain', copyright © Grace Nichols, 1988; 'Granny, Granny Please Comb My Hair', copyright © Grace Nichols, 1984. Reproduced with permission of Curtis Brown Group Ltd, London on behalf of Grace Nichols. • Judith Nicholls: 'Who's There?' from *Midnight Forest* (Faber and Faber Ltd, 1985) reprinted by permission of Faber and Faber Ltd. • James Reeves: 'Animals' Houses', 'Grim and Gloomy', 'The Magic Seeds' and 'Twenty Six Letters' from *Complete Poems for Children* (Heinemann, 1973), copyright © James Reeves. Reprinted by permission of the James Reeves Estate. • E. V. Rieu: 'Mr Blob' from *Cuckoo Calling* (Methuen). Reprinted by permission of Richard Rieu, Executor of E. V. Rieu. • Michael Rosen: 'Mum'll be coming home today' from *Mind Your Own Business* (André Deutsch, 1974). Reprinted by permission of Scholastic Publications Ltd; 'Busy Day' from *You Tell Me* by Roger McGough and Michael Rosen. Copyright © Michael Rosen, 1979. Published by Viking Kestrel and in Puffin Books. • Carl Sandburg: 'Fog' from *Chicago Poems* by Carl Sandburg. Reprinted by permission of Harcourt Brace & Company. • Ian Serraillier: 'The Tickle Rhyme' from *A Puffin Quartet of Poets*, ed E. Graham, 1958. Reprinted by permission of Anne Serrallier. • Edith Sitwell: 'The King of China's Daughter' from *The Collected Poems* (Sinclair Stevenson). Reprinted by permission of David Higham Associates. • James Stephens: 'The Snare' and 'Seumas Beg' from *Collected Poems* (Macmillan, 1926/1965). Reprinted by permission of The Society of Authors on behalf of the copyright owner, Mrs Iris Wise. • Dylan Thomas: 'Johnnie Crack and Flossie Snail (Captain Cat's Song)' from *Under Milk Wood* (Dent, 1954). Copyright © New Directions Publishing Corp., 1954. Reprinted by permission of David Higham Associates and New Directions Publishing Corp. • J. M. Westrup: 'Flying' from *Come Follow Me* (Evans Brothers, an imprint of HarperCollins Publishers Limited). • William Carlos Williams: 'This is Just to Say' from *Collected Poems 1909-1939 Vol I*, copyright © New Directions Publishing Corp. 1938. Reprinted by permission of New Directions Publishing Corp. and Carcanet Press Ltd. • Kit Wright: 'Bluebells and Penguins', 'The Frozen Man' and 'Our Hamster's Life' from *Rabbiting On* (Fontana Lions, an imprint of HarperCollins Publishers Ltd, 1978); 'Song Sung by a Man on a Barge' from *Hot Dog and Other Poems* by Kit Wright, copyright © Kit Wright, 1981. Published by Kestrel Books, Penguin Group.